How to Plan for the School Year

The Elementary Teacher's Essential Guidebook

Deborah Coughlin

HEINEMANN
Portsmouth, NH

Heinemann
A division of Reed Elsevier Inc.
361 Hanover Street
Portsmouth, NH 03801–3912
www.heinemann.com

Offices and agents throughout the world

Library of Congress Cataloging-in-Publication Data
Coughlin, Deborah.
　How to plan for the school year : the elementary teacher's essential guidebook / Deborah Coughlin.
　　　　p.　cm.
Includes bibliographical references and index.
　　ISBN 0-325-00318-1 (alk. paper)
　1.　Elementary school teaching—Handbooks, manuals, etc.
2. Curriculum planning—Handbooks, manuals, etc.　　3.　Classroom management—Handbooks, manuals, etc.　I.　Title.
　LB1555　.C74　2002
　372.1102—dc21　　　　　　　　　　　　　　　　　　　2002004505

Editor: Lois Bridges
Production editor: Sonja S. Chapman
Cover design: Jenny Jensen Greenleaf
Typesetter: Drawing Board Studios
Manufacturing: Steve Bernier

Printed in the United States of America on acid-free paper
06　05　04　03　02　VP　1　2　3　4　5

For Kelly and Dan
with love

Contents

Contents

Forms:

Acknowledgments

I wish to thank:

My editor, Lois Bridges, for her never-ending patience, enthusiasm, encouragement, support, insight, and kindness.

My husband Dan, for his hours of proofreading, brainstorming, and editing.

My multiage K/1 student, Aram Hebert (age 6), for allowing me both the pleasure and the privilege of including his first published piece in this text.

And my parents, who have always encouraged me to dream.

Thank you

Introduction:

Welcome to the New School Year

I love the beginning of the school year. It is a time of excitement and promise. Each year affords me the opportunity to reflect upon my practice and improve my methods. I revisit my philosophies, critically evaluate previous years of teaching, write a new curriculum, and create new learning environments. I get to handle new supplies, work in newly cleaned classrooms, and employ new ideas. My classroom floors shine and smell like wax, my plan book is clean, centers are organized, and all of the nametags on the desks are newly applied and unwrinkled.

Preplanning is exciting and fun. Yet it can also be anxiety-ridden, busy, and involved. I know that the decisions and choices I make prior to the opening of school will set the tone and establish my foundation for the entire school year. This time period is critical. But where do I begin?

Each new year I am accompanied by lists upon lists of items I need to consider, rethink, and remember. There are short-term goals and long-term goals. If I am switching grade levels or beginning at a new school site, then my lists become longer and my work more difficult and time-consuming. Writing my curriculum, individualizing instruction, and learning my grade-level content is simply the tip of the iceberg. Much goes on behind the scenes that affects my teaching. The more I can plan and anticipate, the more effective I can become.

While some areas of teaching are both grade-level and school-site-specific, there are numerous generalities and constants for which I can plan. These preliminary foundations represent the thought processes and areas of teaching I need to have in place before the children arrive. They are also the focus of this book. I invite you to travel with me as I begin to plan for my new school year. Together, we will

- write our curriculum, design a language arts program, and create integrated thematic units
- look at the scheduling of a typical school day
- look at our classrooms to determine the design of our physical setting based upon our grade level, teaching styles, and needs
- establish our classroom management procedures and set up our record-keeping systems
- focus upon evaluation, assessment, accountability, and establishing grades
- discuss building community and examine why the first month of school needs to differ from the rest of the school year
- anticipate and plan for the remainder of the year
- ensure that we have considered all school-site responsibilities and procedures that affect the children and the running of our classrooms.

Creating a classroom structure that accommodates the school system and meets the needs of twenty-five or more individual students is vital, difficult, and time-consuming. The foundation that we establish in our preplanning will allow us to negotiate curriculum, revisit our practices and philosophies, and adapt to various school situations and children. All of these considerations must be in place before that first bell of school rings. Once the children arrive, we need to have our attention turned to them and our teaching. The more prepared we are, the more effective and confident we will be. This is an exciting time of year. It is full of new possibilities and responsibilities.

Are you ready to begin? First, we'll work on writing and organizing our curriculum, and then we'll go look at our new classroom!

1

Writing a Yearlong Integrated Curriculum

Writing a yearlong integrated curriculum is a very time-consuming, complex, and rewarding endeavor. However, it is not an impossible one. By the end of this chapter, we will

- understand the rationale, factors, and criteria involved in creating a yearlong, integrated curriculum
- organize, establish, and write our own yearly theme.

First, we'll begin with an understanding of why writing yearly themes is so important. As we'll see, themes are more than just integrating content. They are one of the most effective ways to meet individual needs, abilities, and curriculum accountabilities. Integrated themes also allow for depth of content rather than a general surface coverage of subskills and facts and provide for reinforcement of concepts from varying perspectives and domains. We will begin exploring integrated themes by looking at some commonly asked questions.

Why Write a Yearlong Integrated Curriculum?

The reason we write a yearlong theme is to make the learning of new knowledge sequential, logical, and more understandable for the children.

We are looking at all of our grade-level skills and expectations and pulling them together into a sensible, tidy context that flows naturally. We are providing the transition from one skill to the next by transferring, making, and strengthening the connections between the separate content skills and presenting these skills in an integrated format applicable to the children's everyday lives.

Because we are organizing the material for the children into a logical sequence that combines multiple skills, we are simultaneously presenting new knowledge, reinforcing old knowledge, creating schema, and building upon existing and beginning concepts. Because we are modeling the application of these skills through everyday experiences, the children will be immersed in their learning, and the curriculum will be predominantly hands-on, with experiences that relate to their everyday lives.

Much thought, reflection, creativity, and preplanning goes into the creation of a theme. We are processing, transferring, integrating, planning, designing, and scaffolding our yearlong game plan. We need to be thoughtful, accountable, and thorough.

Why Not Use the Textbook Curriculum?

One of the major reasons that I can't follow the textbook curriculum is that there simply is not enough time in a day, week, or school year to implement the various suggested textbook materials necessary to complete all the units of study thoroughly within the intended scope and sequence to provide for understanding and deeper learning.

The second reason I can't utilize the various content textbooks is that the textbook companies work in isolation. Therefore, I may be expected to teach content in isolation that would lend itself to seamless integration into lessons of various unrelated subjects. I would not be able to provide a logical sequence—a bridge from the new to the known—utilize recent schemata, or show the connectedness, relevancy, and authenticity of the curriculum to our everyday lives. The concept of "the circle of life" and all things being interrelated and dependent upon one another is lost in this chopped-up form.

The third reason is that I believe teaching that is directed by the textbooks does not take into account the children, the culture, or research on sound teaching. In fact:

- Textbooks are often very limited in their coverage of the content, depth, and perspectives represented.
- One textbook will not meet the academic, reading, and developmental needs of every student.
- Textbooks are usually not current.
- Textbooks cannot be negotiated to our students' interests, inquiries, abilities, or experiences.

4

- Textbooks use expository writing that forces students to utilize different reading skills and strategies than narrative text; it is less familiar to the children, and therefore more difficult to read than narrative text.
- Textbooks supply facts and details, while literature and various other forms of print surround the academic concepts with personal stories and context that relate to the reader and involve the students in their learning.
- Literature and various types of print expose the reader to different and needed reading opportunities and strategies that short excerpts found in textbooks do not. Narrative stories maintain plot development, carry a story line over time, utilize cause-and-effect relationships, demonstrate character development, encourage prediction, illustrate sequencing, and generate interest.

Research also shows that we remember best and learn more when we are taught through stories. When given a name and face, events and experiences become personal, involving the reader in the character's life and circumstances. It gives the reader ownership of the problem and a real desire to find a solution. This type of teaching leads to expression of personal and creative thought, predicting, problem solving, critical thinking, self-expression, valuing of ideas, tolerance, and engagement with print.

Therefore, if the school where we teach mandates the sole use of textbooks, and textbooks are the only resource material available to us, then we will need to use the texts to write our curriculum as needed. We will supplement our textbooks and curriculum with literature from our public or private libraries.

What Are the Criteria for Writing a Theme?

When writing a yearlong integrated curriculum or theme, we must consider all academic and social factors. Our curriculum needs to meet six criteria. The first three are as follows:

> Criterion 1: Incorporate and integrate all mandated and required standards, benchmarks, and tested material for all content areas.
> Criterion 2: Consider developmental approximations of our students.
> Criterion 3: Consider social and cultural issues affecting our students.

In this chapter we are going to focus upon these three criteria of writing an integrated curriculum. These criteria are used when actually writing a theme. They teach us *how* to write an integrated unit.

The remaining three are applied to our theme once it is written. It is a way of verifying or checking our theme to determine whether it is functional, logical, and sound. The last three criteria will be addressed in Chapter 2, when we are further along with the creation of our theme.

What Do We Need to Know Before We Begin?

To write a yearlong integrated theme, we need to know our required curriculum and the amount of autonomy allowed at our school site. Some schools require teachers to follow the various district-adopted textbook series, in sequence, as their curriculum. Others allow teachers to use textbooks as reference material, while some schools do not use textbooks at all.

What is the required curricular program at your school site? The required curricular program will include all of the school, district, state, and federal requirements that students need to know at each established grade level. These requirements are referred to by such names as *standards*, *benchmarks*, *grade-level expectations*, and/or *essential elements of instruction*. The required curricular program at your school will determine how we need to plan our curriculum.

Additionally, we also need to know the standardized tests and the district required assessments the students at our grade level take throughout the year (along with their approximate dates).

How Do We Identify Our Required Curriculum?

To identify required curriculum, we need to gather all of our content benchmarks and test materials for our grade level. These will be based upon the federal, state, district, and school standards. These standards may change from state to state, district to district, and school to school. To locate your required curriculum, check your school employee handbook, ask your curriculum coordinator in your school or at the district level, retrieve the information from your district's website, ask fellow teachers, gather textbooks and resource materials, and look at information for parents put out by the district relating what children are required to learn at each grade level.

Taking all of our resources, and one content area at a time, we list all of the stated benchmarks, standards, concepts, skills, and subskills the children are required to learn. Use a separate sheet of paper for every content area. When we are finished we will have multiple sheets of paper containing all of the standards we are required to teach and that the children are accountable for learning, by content area.

How Do We Organize a Yearlong Integrated Curriculum?

A yearlong integrated curriculum is organized by taking all of our required curriculum, integrating the content concepts, and coming up with a yearly theme. From our yearly theme we choose four subcategories that support this main theme. Each subcategory will then become a quarterly focus.

Once our yearly and quarterly themes are established, we determine what content will be taught during each quarter. Then, we take our quarterly content and break it down into weekly and daily lesson plans.

Sample Theme: Primary

The following is a sample outline of a primary (K–2) yearlong theme based upon required curriculum:

Yearlong Theme *Spaces and Places*

- Quarter 1 Theme: *Places Around Us*
  a. classroom community
  b. community products and services
  c. wants and needs
  d. school and classroom procedures
  e. safety rules and procedures

- Quarter 2 Theme: *Underground Spaces*
  a. insects, worms, ants
  b. underground habitats
  c. creatures that burrow
  d. plants and seeds

- Quarter 3 Theme: *Up-Above Places*
  a. Earth as our home planet
  b. solar system
  c. constellations
  d. Sun as a star
  e. measurement

- Quarter 4 Theme: *Spooky Spaces*
  a. fairy tale genre study
  b. the woods as setting
  c. nocturnal animals
  d. contrast/comparison
  e. letter writing
  f. characters
  g. inference

Sample Theme: Intermediate

The following intermediate (Grades 3–6) sample theme utilizes the same yearly theme (Spaces and Places) as outlined in the primary sample. The only difference between the intermediate theme and the primary theme is that the headings are now tailored to accommodate the required intermediate benchmarks and standards.

Yearlong Theme: *Spaces and Places*

- Quarter 1 Theme: *Spaces and Places Around Us*
  a. tells how our lives are affected by land, climate, vegetation, and other resources
  b. explains the rights and responsibilities of a consumer
  c. describes the role of citizen in government
  d. tells how governments make and enforce laws
  e. compares types of government
  f. tells how countries depend upon each other economically
  g. explains recycling
  h. tells how human behavior and technology affect the environment, ecosystems, and humankind
  i. knows that living things have systems that control reproduction, growth, and health
  j. shows how ecosystems work
  k. tells how nonliving matter and energy affect ecosystems
  l. reads and discusses a variety of literature
  m. recognizes a theme common to several stories
  n. writes clearly and supports ideas

- Quarter 2 Theme: *Changing Places*
  a. tells how early civilizations in the Western Hemisphere affected later American civilizations
  b. compares how colonies developed in the Western Hemisphere
  c. tells how nations changed after colonial rule
  d. describes how technology and change affect a nation's economy
  e. understands events in history by using time-lines
  f. locates major cities of the western world
  g. locates and discusses the political boundaries of the countries in the Western Hemisphere
  h. understands the history of Earth using geological records
  i. creates presentations for an audience
  j. uses footnotes, bibliographies, visual aids, newspapers, and technology

- Quarter 3 Theme: *Faraway Spaces*
    a. describes the size and movement of planets, satellites, asteroids, and comets
    b. discusses the makeup of the universe
    c. knows all matter is affected by gravity
    d. tells how the environment and Earth's forces affect plants and animals
    e. explains the use of the international dateline and time zones
    f. uses science, math, and social studies vocabulary in reading, writing, and speaking

- Quarter 4 Theme: *Energetic Places*
    a. describes an atom
    b. describes how energy is used in technology
    c. describes an electromagnetic spectrum and how it is used
    d. describes the properties of waves
    e. discusses the use of natural resources to provide energy
    f. tells how environment and Earth's forces affect plants and animals
    g. uses reading skills to detect meaning from text

How Do We Choose a Yearlong Theme?

To choose a yearlong theme, we take all of our various content requirements and search for commonalities or threads among the different content standards. To do this creatively, we think about how, when, and where these standards are used and applied. Under what circumstances, context, or setting do we utilize the required skill? Is there a relationship or connection between various content standards?

We then brainstorm, reorganize, and categorize the content benchmarks by sorting and listing them according to their similarities or their relationships to each other. Next, we look at our groups of related concepts and apply a title or name to each group.

After we have named all of our related groups, we take the titles of each group and list them together. Now, working with just our group titles, we search for a way in which they can be connected, applied, or placed in a context where they occur. This requires a lot of thought, creativity, and outside-the-box thinking. Think about when or how people use these skills in everyday life. Maybe a setting or location like the woods or our neighborhood can tie together these groups. Perhaps our common thread between groups could be an emotion or a relationship, like friendship.

We want to end up with one umbrella heading that integrates the content of all of our required groupings. This heading now becomes our yearlong theme— our common thread uniting requirements and our content focus. Our curriculum will be designed around this theme, and the environment and decor of our room will reflect and support our chosen focus.

How Do We Choose Our Quarterly Content?

Once we have our yearlong theme and our related content groupings, we need to go back and look at our groups. In order to create our quarterly content and/or theme, we need to take these groups and narrow them down to only four major groups. The reason we want only four groupings is because each group will now represent the theme and content for each of the four quarters of the school year.

Once we have determined our four categories, we look at our chosen groupings to decide the sequence of our four themes. To do this, we will need our yearly calendar and our yearly testing schedule.

Our first choice for arranging our quarterly themes is to apply the natural flow and sequence of our thematic units. We will need to look at our school calendar to see if the dates are appropriate for the theme, and if there is any testing done during that quarter.

If the order of the themes is not relevant, we may want to work solely around our school calendar and our testing dates. For example, if we know that our students have a major writing exam in the spring, then our focus for that quarter should incorporate knowledge and activities that will support the practice of their writing. All of these issues must be considered.

Is There a Difference Between Writing a Primary Theme and an Intermediate Theme?

No. Regardless of the elementary grade we teach, we follow the same thought processes and procedures for writing our yearlong integrated theme and quarterly themes. Our writing and organization procedures will not change.

What will change, for me, is the curriculum focus I will give to the thematic units. In the primary grades of K–3, I like my yearly themes to revolve primarily around the required science curriculum content. In grades 4–6, I like my yearly themes to revolve primarily around the required social study curriculum.

Why Do My Primary Themes Focus Mainly Upon Science?

In the primary grades of K–3, I write my themes around the required science content because it is not usually necessary to intentionally focus upon the required social studies content. Almost everything the students do in the younger grades supports a social studies concept. By simply coming to school and learning to navigate their worlds, the children are already incorporating and applying most of their required social studies skills and criteria.

Yet the science concepts do not apply themselves so obviously and incidentally. Therefore, when I teach younger children, my thematic unit will be science-based and our classroom environment will reflect this in the decor. All other content areas (social studies, language arts, math) will be integrated and applied through the lens of this theme.

Why Do My Intermediate Themes Focus Primarily Upon Social Studies?

In the older grades my yearlong themes revolve around the social studies content. I find that in the intermediate grades, the social studies content requires a more direct focus of attention and contains curriculum (such as history) that is not experienced in the students' normal daily activities. Unlike the primary grades, where the content is mostly incidental, functional, and social knowledge, the intermediate grades require testing of specific knowledge that needs to be internalized, grasped, demonstrated, and understood.

Therefore, in the intermediate grades, I begin writing the curriculum with the required skills from the social studies benchmarks. Our theme will be social studies–based and all other subject areas will be integrated into our social studies unit. Additionally, most of the social studies will be taught predominantly through literature and literature discussion groups, inquiry groups, presentations, projects, and some direct teaching.

The science will be integrated as much as possible and the concepts will be introduced and applied as they become relevant to the studied social studies era or region. Any areas of science that I am unable to integrate will be taught through inquiry studies and some direct teaching.

What About Language Arts and Math?

It's important to remember that the language arts include reading, writing, listening, and speaking. It will be difficult to teach any of our other subject areas or content without utilizing one or more of these four domains. Therefore, skills required in the language arts can easily and naturally be incorporated into all of the other content areas.

Rather than think of them as separate content, we can use our language arts skills in combination with our other requirements. For example, an intermediate science inquiry project could be used for evaluating the required science benchmarks. It could also be used to evaluate grammar, spelling, the writing process, reading for information, outlining, research skills, library skills, computer skills, public speaking, and listening.

In the primary grades, emergent readers require a more direct focus with the teaching of the language arts, particularly reading and writing. The key is to teach the language art skills using materials (fiction and nonfiction) that support and teach our theme. We may read and write about friendship, the Moon, frogs, and so on.

The math concepts will be taught and integrated primarily as they occur in our everyday life. Whether we teach primary or intermediate grades, our students apply skills related to measuring, counting, directionality, money, symmetry, fractions, patterning, problem solving, using a calendar, concepts of greater than and less than, telling time, and basic computation in the everyday context of their environment.

Next, we look for ways to integrate our math into our yearlong theme. How are these math skills utilized, or how can these math skills help us find out more information about our study?

Our next possibility is to try to connect the math to a piece of literature, poetry, or song. If there are math requirements that can't be integrated, they must be taught separately and in isolation from our theme. We do not skip math because we cannot create a way to integrate the concept. We simply schedule a separate math time each day to teach the required curriculum as necessary. We can't fit everything. We do the best we can. And, as we gain confidence, experience, and trust in the application of a theme, we will find it easier to integrate more and more material across the curricular board.

Is There a Difference Between *Integration* and *Coordination?*

Yes. In fact, a common error made in writing a theme is not distinguishing between *coordination* and *integration*. Let's take an imaginary yearlong integrated theme of Into the Woods. During this year we may decide to take one quarter to focus upon hibernation or various animals found in the woods. Because bears are included on these lists, we could decide to cover our theme of bears by

- counting bear
- making bear cookies.

Although these are great math ideas, they are activities that teach us nothing about the nature of bears or hibernation. Counting bears and making bear cookies are not benchmarks required by the state or district, and rarely do we have a reason to count bears in our daily lives.

These activities are *coordinated*, not *integrated*. We are not teaching anything directly about the subject of our theme: bears/hibernation. However, we could choose one of the following activities instead:

- investigating and counting the combs in a beehive
- graphing the various types of bears
- graphing and making our favorite honey snack
- counting the days of hibernation and creating a ratio or percent relating days of hibernation to days in a year
- counting the different animals that hibernate
- comparing and contrasting *migration* with *hibernation.*

Now we are *integrating* graphing, measuring, counting, and migration into our study of bears. This topic could certainly flow naturally into a discussion of the four seasons. Integration of concepts allows us to learn more than one skill at the same time we are learning more about the topic we are studying.

What if We Can't Integrate Some Required Content?

Sometimes our required curriculum will make it difficult to integrate content areas. For instance, if we are required to teach the Revolutionary War and the rain forest, then we will be hard-pressed to create a commonality to allow integration.

We could treat the rain forest as an inquiry project in science that would separate it from our theme. Or, we could decide to teach a lesson on contrast and comparison by talking about the terrains in the Northeast that differ from the rain forest. And, we could even brainstorm how the war would have been fought differently had it been in rain forest territory.

Concepts difficult to integrate may also be utilized to support or teach writing workshop, research writing, public speaking, and/or test-taking skills. It's a good idea to look at our school calendar to seek out school weeks that are shortened because of vacations or workshops. These are not good times to begin a new theme study. They may, however, be a perfect time to teach a mini-lesson or unit on any of the concepts we could not integrate thematically.

Why Do We Let Our Benchmarks Generate Our Themes?

It is important that we begin generating and determining our theme by starting with the required content benchmarks. (When using the term *benchmarks*, I am inclusively referring to the broad base of sequences, standards, assessments, and grade-level expectations decided upon by each state, district, and school.) These drive our curriculum. We must know that we are presenting every standard for which the children and we are accountable. We need to study our benchmarks and seek out the natural patterns, continuity, and connections that exist between these random skills so that we can group them authentically.

It is a very common and understandable decision to first create some thematic topics and then attempt to fit the required curriculum skills into these predetermined headings. But it is a mistake. By creating our thematic headings first, and then trying to fit our skills into these predetermined themes, we are negating and overlooking the natural connections and commonalities among the various content skills. We must let the benchmarks inform us and let the connections between our requirements suggest the groupings.

What About Multiage Classrooms?

Writing a yearly theme for multiage classrooms is really easier than it sounds. We are working with two years of benchmarks. But by looking at the benchmarks, we will see that there is much overlap and continuation of concepts from one school year to the next, especially in the early years. Many of the benchmark concepts are quite broad and differ from year to year only in depth of content or developmental expectations. Because we will be working with two *grade levels* in one classroom, we will have double the textbook resources and the authority and flexibility for meeting each student's individual needs. Schoolwork in multiage classrooms is designed around a student's instructional level rather than the school calendar or grade level. Each child works at his own pace while reaching for the same goals as his peers. Therefore, teaching multiage is nothing less than what we should be doing in every classroom. Every class or grade level is functioning under the same circumstances of academic and social variability. The difference with multiage is that this variability is expected, recognized, and supported.

Now that we've discussed some common questions, it may be helpful to view some samples of thematic units before we begin to write our own yearly plan. The samples I share here are merely excerpts from examples of themes. They are ideas and starting points to get our creative juices flowing. They are neither thorough nor complete units of study.

Sample Primary Themes

The following are science benchmarks that we need to organize into an overall theme.

The students will

- understand that vibrations produce sound
- identify the habits of healthy people
- discuss ways animals and plants rely on each other
- classify an item by two attributes.

Let's apply these science concepts into three different primary units of study, or yearly themes: The Farm, The Meadow, and Fairy Tales.

The Farm

There is a great working farm within field-trip distance of our school that the children love. I'd like to do that field trip this year. If my yearly theme revolves around farms, then we could focus upon the ways that plants and animals rely on each other on the farm. We could follow the circle of life scenarios evident between plants, animals, and humans.

I addition, we could look at the products of the farm and use the book *Gregory the Terrible Eater* (Sharmat 1989) to move the conversation from life cycles toward good nutrition and health. Using the basic food groups, we could move into our five senses and explore taste, and include our requirement of sound being produced by vibration. A tin-can telephone would tie into the country atmosphere. This would incorporate the concept that sound is produced by vibrations.

This focus would also allow me to teach

- the ways that farms support our community
- plants and seeds
- mothers and their young

- weather conditions for planting
- products and services
- and so on.

A great read-aloud would be *Charlotte's Web* (White 1952). (I may also want to get into the study of spiders, friendship, or weaving.)

The Meadow

We could examine ways that plants, insects, and animals rely on each other in the meadow. This could bring in the concepts of camouflage, prey and predator, food cycles, pollination, and so on. Eric Carle's book *The Very Hungry Caterpillar* (1984) is a perfect segue into the concepts of nutrition. His book *The Very Quiet Cricket* (1997) could introduce us to a discussion of how crickets make their sound through vibration. This focus could lead us into measuring, with Leo Lionni's *Inch By Inch* (1995) and telling time, with another Carle book, *The Very Grouchy Ladybug* (1996).

Great read-alouds to incorporate nutrition would be Roald Dahl's *James and the Giant Peach* (1996) and *Charlie and the Chocolate Factory* (1998). Other favorite read-alouds incorporating insects would be *Cricket in Times Square (Seldon 1970), Beetles Lightly Toasted* (Naylor 1989), and *How to Eat Fried Worms* (Rockwell 1953).

Fairy Tales

Most fairy tales are set in the woods. If I wanted to teach fairy tales, I could look at the relationship between plants and animals in the woodlands. We could explore environmental issues in protecting our trees and our forests. We could explore ecosystems. The forest could lead us into a study of birds, migration, nocturnal animals, woodland animals, reptiles, fauna and foliage, habitats, and hibernation. We could

- grow beans with Jack in *Jack and the Beanstalk* and explore the vibrations created by the giant's stomping boots and booming voice
- read *The Jolly Postman* (Ahlberg and Ahlberg 1986) and incorporate letter writing
- read books by Jon Sczieska to examine point of view, fact/opinion, and perspective
- examine nursery rhymes to look at the eating habits and food of nursery rhyme and storybook characters
- read different versions of *Little Red Riding Hood* to study safety and following the rules

16

- work on setting as a story element
- use Venn diagrams and graphic organizers to compare and contrast fairy tales
- study fairy tales as a genre
- create a storybook land as a functional working community.

A great read-aloud would be Roald Dahl's *BFG* (1998).

Sample Intermediate Themes

As with science, social studies themes can vary tremendously depending upon our required content and grade level.

One year our content revolved around the eastern United States. Did you know that two-thirds of all people in the United States are within a day's travel of the Appalachian Trail? That information created an umbrella focus for a yearly theme based upon walking the Appalachian Trail. I contacted trail officials to obtain maps and guidebooks and integrated the material into my required benchmarks and standards. Throughout the school year, we "walked" the Appalachian Trail.

To begin, we measured and logged the distance that our class walks daily between our usual school activities and destinations. After retrieving a daily walking average, we started to map out our trek at the beginning of the trail, in Georgia. Daily we charted our miles up the trail map. Our goal was to reach the end of the trail, in Maine, by June.

As we moved up the trail we learned about the geology, fauna, wildlife, history, and customs of each area. We planned for our trek by learning about outdoor survival, building shelters, eating foods from the environment, making dyes from plants, and first aid.

Throughout the year we created replicas of Appalachian crafts and quilting. We learned how to weave and sew, and at the end of the school year we sponsored an Appalachian Craft Fair for the school and parents. Our fair raised more than a thousand dollars, which we donated to the Appalachian Trail for its restoration projects.

Another year, the social study content focused around the Colonial period, the Revolutionary War, and the Civil War. Using historical fiction and/or nonfiction novels as the primary reading program, the students presented projects and reenactments of events, searched for forts and maps, created time lines, and located and investigated the accuracy of the historical data presented.

The students and their families worked together to investigate and write their own family *histories*, biographies, and autobiographies. Every month the students and their families would gather back at school for an evening of family storytelling. We would gather together, read our stories, eat cake, and learn about each other's lives.

Now that we have a few examples of what a theme could look like, we are ready to create our own yearlong theme for our own required content areas.

Writing a Yearlong Theme

Gather the Necessary Materials

To begin you will need

- all district curriculum guidelines for your grade level
- all state standards or benchmarks that pertain to your grade level
- a list of all of the required assessments for your grade level and what content they cover
- the teacher editions and resource materials for every adopted content-area textbook at your grade level
- knowledge of the depth of coverage and content material taught in the grades before and after the grades you teach
- knowledge of developmental approximations and expectations based upon your class population and grade level
- general knowledge of the social and cultural interests of the children you teach
- a list of things you would like to teach
- knowledge of available resources and materials
- pencils
- an eraser
- lots of paper.

Ready?

Start with the Benchmarks and Standards

Looking at your state and district curriculum requirements, write down all of the required content material to be covered this year for your grade level. List each content area separately (math, science, social studies, etc.). Then, go through and write down all of the sub-skills and benchmarks required for each subject/content area (don't forget to include secondary content areas, such as health, computer science, physical education, etc.) For example, the following is a sampling of the benchmarks that are required of first-grade students in my school district.

Reading
- use background knowledge in responding to literature
- use decoding skills
- use simple reference materials
- read simple directions to perform tasks
- understand *setting*

Writing
- write for a variety of purposes
- write legibly (neatly)
- recognize letter-sound associations for consonants
- plan by brainstorming, discussing, drawing

Math
- count to one hundred
- count money to fifty cents using pennies, nickels, dimes, and quarters
- identify two-dimensional shapes and relate them to the real world
- tell time to the hour and half hour
- write numerals ten through nineteen

Science
- classify various objects by shape and color
- describe daily habits people should practice to maintain good health
- describe ways plants and animals rely on each other
- use vibration to produce sound

Social Studies
- give or identify full name, address, and phone number
- identify and describe various jobs in the community
- understand how people depend upon and use community services
- give examples of rules that keep a neighborhood and school safe

The required content curriculum for your theme will be dependent upon your school district and assigned grade level.

Record All Tested Content

Look at all required assessments and write down the test objectives, formats, concepts, and content covered.

In the primary grades we mostly deal with district-required reading material assessments and the state and national norm-referenced tests of achievement that assess general grade-level knowledge in all subject areas. In the intermediate grades we may be looking at state writing exams and national standardized measures, both norm- and criterion-referenced instruments.

Required Reading Tests

The required reading tests are usually derived from the district's adopted reading textbook series, commonly referred to as a basal series. The test is usually created by the reading series company and can be located in either the teacher's resource book or the test manuals. Each district and school has its individual criteria for which tests need to be completed and/or introduced, but usually the classroom teacher is required to have a reading test sample from the beginning, middle, and end of the school year. This usually transfers into making sure that, at a minimum, our students have completed the required theme tests and readings that need to be recorded in their cumulative folders.

It is important that you now familiarize yourself with the content on these tests, and every test your students will be taking. You want to know what they are required to learn and what you are accountable for teaching. You also want to list the testing requirements along with the content requirements so that you can integrate them into your yearly theme as well.

If the topics you need to teach do not mesh with your content study, it is okay. You can then plan on teaching the tests for a different purpose. You can use them to provide direct instructional time in test-taking skills, reading for detail, writing to a prompt, story elements, and reading test formats. Because many of the reading textbook companies assess the required nationally tested standards, the instruments are all quite similar in their content and format.

- Most reading tests include skills such as asking a student to read a title of a story and look at its accompanying picture. Stemming from this activity, the student is then requested to write a prediction about what the story could be about.
- Comprehension is frequently assessed by the child's ability to follow character development, plot development, or sequencing over a short period of time. The students predominantly are asked to write, draw, circle a picture, choose from a multiple-choice item, or provide a short-answer response for a reply.

- Inferential questions can be determined by the stories' text and illustrations.
- Phonemic awareness, spelling, and skills of convention are generally handled through multiple-choice formats.
- There is usually some type of a letter or a newspaper article that the children need to edit for convention.
- The tests generally end with a reader response section, which is not usually scored.

You need to prepare your children for these various test formats, as well as the tested materials.

Textbooks

Next, go through all of the adopted textbooks and available teaching resources. This is for two purposes. The first is to identify all of the objectives that the adopted textbook tells you to teach. In the beginning of each chapter, and prior to each lesson, there is a section that usually tells you about the chapter's content and contains a list of the concepts, skills, or information that will be introduced. You need to copy down all of the objectives for every textbook.

When you are finished, you will have a list of all the objectives the district textbooks are reported to teach and cover. Note that the list of textbook content and objectives may not align with your district's required benchmarks. In fact, they could be completely different. This is not atypical. But it is confusing.

The first thing to do is verify that the required benchmarks you are using are up to date. Then find out if the students are accountable for the benchmark content, the textbook content, or both. You need to be clear as to what it is you should be teaching.

Some schools do not utilize textbooks so their textbook resources are often outdated and not current to the new benchmarks or grade-level expectations. Sometimes the material filtered down through the district regarding benchmarks is inaccurate or misunderstood. If in doubt, call the curriculum specialist at your district to see what guidelines and requirements you are to follow.

Add this list to the list of your district and state requirements. This list can help provide ideas for mini-lessons, individual instruction, and/or inquiry projects.

The second reason to go through the textbooks is to establish available teaching materials. You want to make sure that you have the resources to teach your created curriculum. You'll need to look through all textbook manuals and resource aids. You'll also look through literature sets, leveled book sets, poetry, songs, games, magazines, picture books, professional books, science and math supplies, community resources, and media supplies.

Research the Grade-Level Content

We need to have an idea of the content coverage and materials in the grades before and after the grade we teach. We need to start our children where they are comfortable in their learning and connect the new to the known. To do this, we need to know where they are going and where they have been.

Consider Developmental Approximations

We need to know the developmental approximations of our students at this grade level. We need to be familiar with developmental stages of literacy and learning so that we can form some expectations regarding the developmental levels and interests of the students we teach, and we need to make sure that we begin where everybody can be successful.

Using stages of approximate development we can determine a fairly good starting point for lessons and instructional materials. These whole-class generalizations will be continuously fine-tuned to individual children as time goes by. As we learn each child better, we will be able to speak to her specific demonstrated performances and areas of strengths, weaknesses, and interests.

Think About Social and Cultural Issues

What TV shows do your students like? Who are their heroes? What are their interests? What is their home life like? What worries do they have when they leave the classroom? Who supports them at home? How can they relate to your curriculum? Who will have materials to complete their schoolwork? Do they have money for field trips? Do they have money for lunch? What are the family expectations and goals for your children?

Every single element in our children's being will affect their education and their learning. The more we know about our students, the more we can adapt our teaching to accommodate and support their needs.

A curriculum that employs many structures, yet remains flexible and open-ended, allows us to establish whole-class procedures, routines, and expectations while individualizing instruction. That's what we're working toward.

And individualizing instruction also includes accommodating the personal interests and enjoyments of the teacher and the children. Curriculum needs to be engaging and interesting if it is to be nurtured and grow.

List Things You Want to Teach

Now that you have a list of all of the required things to think about, let's create a list of the things that you would have fun teaching. Include the things that you think your children would also like to learn. For example:

a. lizards
b. Abraham Lincoln
c.
d.
e.

When all required content, assessments, textbooks, developmental, social, and cultural considerations are listed, you are ready to move on.

Choose a Yearlong Theme

Primary
Now, look at the required skills and benchmarks that you listed for just the science content. My primary theme will derive from these science concepts only, as I explained earlier. Some teachers may prefer to organize around math or language arts. The philosophy and process does not change. Organize around the content area you feel is most adaptable to your needs.) Your job now is to integrate and analyze these science concepts (or whichever focus you chose) to come up with one all-encompassing commonality, or category. For example, if you need to teach weather, plants, and animals that lay eggs, you could integrate and teach these concepts through the theme of cycles: the water cycle, the cycle of a seed, and the life cycle of chickens. Cycles then becomes your theme.

Intermediate
Now, look at the required skills and benchmarks that you listed for just the social studies content. My intermediate themes work best when they are derived from the social studies concepts. Again, your job is to integrate and analyze these concepts to come up with one all-encompassing commonality, or category. Usually the social studies content is already organized around geographical regions or historical events. This makes integrating and identifying your yearlong theme a little easier. Your theme could simply be Colonization or The Western Hemisphere.

Create Quarterly Themes

Connecting All Required Content to Your Yearlong Theme
Now, go back to all of your listed content skills from earlier in this chapter (see "Gather the Necessary Materials" and "Start with the Benchmarks and Standards," earlier in the chapter). This time you are going to look at all of the required skills in every subject area to determine how the various concepts fit together, fit into, or apply to your yearlong theme. If your theme is Cycles, look to see how each content concept (math, language arts, etc.) relates to and can be taught under the umbrella of Cycles.

Organizing Concepts

Next, by removing the skills from their content headings and reorganizing them into different categories, look for the commonalities and connections among all of the content concepts. You want to see how many similar groups you have, as well as observe how you can connect these groups to the theme of Cycles.

A good way to find common threads among benchmarks is to create Venn diagrams, webs, or graphic organizers (see sample organizers in Figures 1–1 and 1–2). What are the skills or concepts that can be grouped together or flow to-gether naturally? Keep looking for overlaps, connections, and possibilities. Can they be connected by their application, an author study, a genre, a piece of litera-ture, or even a setting? Can they be compared or contrasted?

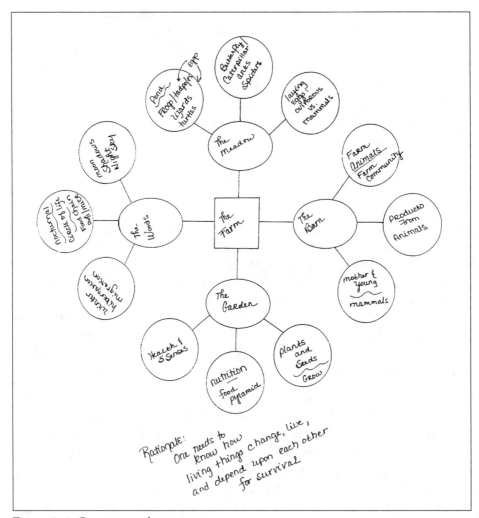

Figure 1–1. Organizing subject concepts

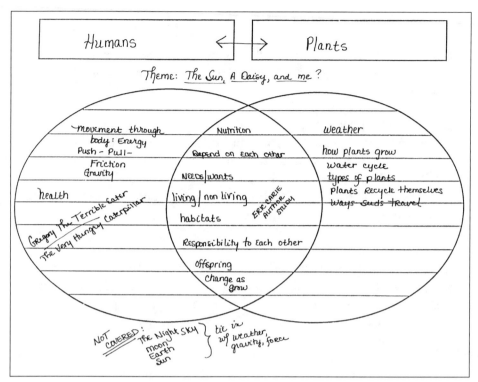

Figure 1–2. Organizing thematic concepts

You want to come up with at least five or six different possible ways for your con-cepts and skills to be grouped and/or linked together and to your theme. This will be a time-consuming, but informative adventure. You want to discover and determine that you have exhausted all options in rearranging your concepts.

Narrowing Down Content Categories
When you have your groups of content categories, you need to narrow them down to your four best choices. By best, I mean the most thorough and logical in their support of your theme, application, and natural flow of sequence. These four categories now become your subthemes and content for each quarter.

Sequencing Quarters
Now, looking at your four quarterly themes, you need to decide which category to teach during which quarter. I usually decide based upon the natural sequence or flow from one skill to the other, or I use the calendar to look for a seasonal connection, a holiday connection, a field trip connection, or a school-related connection. If it doesn't matter, I simply choose my order randomly.

Adding Content Not Thematically Integrated

Once you have your yearlong theme and quarterly focus determined, you need to go back to your content lists of skills. These must be taught somewhere. Look over your yearly outline and plug in necessary content and skills where they best fit or are needed.

Adding Content You Want to Teach

When all skills are accounted for, it is your time to incorporate the material and concepts that you would like to teach, and/or the topics that the children are interested in. Look at your established themes. You are searching for ways that your desired content can be connected to your established required content. Add them under the appropriate quarter.

Finalizing Your Theme

Finally, go back one more time. Look to see how complete your study is. Is it thorough? United? Logical? What else do you need to include to enhance or support your required content? Fill in the gaps and place additional content under the appropriate quarter. Ask yourself the following questions:

Is my theme logical and accountable? Does it provide for sound learning?
Do I (or the school) have the money and/or the materials to support this curriculum?
Can I readily incorporate the theme into a decor and classroom setting?

If the answers are yes, then you are finished. If not, you may want to go back and rethink your decisions. Creating a theme under the best of circumstances is time-consuming and expensive. It is a process that is built upon each year. You must make sure this is the direction you wish to take before you begin investing either time or money.

TEACHER'S NOTE: It is a good idea to make copies of the required benchmarks and standards, along with all given testing schedules. Keep this copy in your lesson plan book. As you teach each concept, document the number in your plan book next to that lesson. On your benchmark forms, fill in the dates you taught each concept. This provides for excellent documentation and organizational structure.

Conclusion

We have just gone through the process of writing a yearlong theme. We have created

- our integrated yearlong theme
- our thematic study for each quarter of the school year.

A successfully balanced yearlong theme requires experience with the grade level, developmental level, assessments, and content that you teach. It may be wise to work up to yearlong themes by integrating slowly as you feel comfortable. Just like our students, we should not expect to learn and apply so many new concepts at one time. Start little by little. Give yourself time to become comfortable, and experience and see the learning that takes place and the responses from your students.

Start with an activity integrated around a storybook. From there, try a daily theme, a weekly theme, a monthly theme, and so on. The longer you teach the same grade level, the more you will identify further areas of the curriculum that lend themselves to integration. Additionally, you will feel more confident because you will be able to see and trust in the learning that takes place through authentic integration.

In the next chapter, we will continue to work on our yearlong integrated theme. With our scaffolding now in place for writing our yearlong theme, we need to look at how we are going to go about teaching it. Chapter 2 will focus upon our last three criteria:

Criterion 4: Sustain ongoing assessment, individualization, and growth.
Criterion 5: Allow for development of a balanced academic program.
Criterion 6: Allow for immersion in the classroom environment.

2

Completing Your Yearlong Theme

By now we have already decided upon, and outlined, *what* we are going to teach for our yearlong integrated curriculum, we know we have our required content covered, and we know how the required content will fit together.

In this chapter we are going to switch gears a little bit. We are still working on completing our yearlong curriculum, but we can put all of our notes and webs regarding our themes away.

The last three criteria are not specific to our theme. They are applied to every theme and every curriculum, regardless of the title, focus, grade level, or content. These last three criteria relate to *how* we are going to teach the required content and how we are going to immerse it into our classroom environment.

Meeting the Last Three Criteria

With our yearlong integrated theme in place, we need to look at how we are going to meet the remaining three required criteria of our curriculum:

Criterion 4: Sustain ongoing assessment, individualization, and growth.
Criterion 5: Allow for development of a balanced academic program.
Criterion 6: Allow for immersion in the classroom environment.

Now, we need to determine *how* our curriculum, regardless of the theme and content, will identify and assess our students' needs (for both regular and main-streamed children) document periodic and annual growth, individualize instruction, contain successful elements of a balanced literacy curriculum, and be immersed, supported, and reflected through the classroom environment.

These three criteria must be embedded into our daily curriculum so that they are simultaneous, seamless, and continuous throughout the school day. *Every* lesson we teach and *everything* we do in the classroom should allow us to assess student abilities, assess student needs, document student growth, provide individualized instruction and teach a skill or concept within a balanced literacy program, as well as be supported by the classroom environment.

Everything we design for the students must be

- individualized based upon each child's zone of proximal development (ZPD) (Vygotsky 1978)
- flexible enough to accommodate all varying needs and stages of development
- able to inform us about each child's ability, grasp of concept, literacy, and current ZPD.

These elements—individualization, flexibility, and evaluation—must be present in all lessons. Remember: the reason we present lessons and continuously assess is to be able to identify what each student needs so we can start him where he is and lead him ahead in a developmentally appropriate direction. It is these ongoing observations from teaching which provide the fodder for our future curriculum and targeted lessons. The question is how do we do this?

Everything we do must inform us about the child academically and/or socially. As teachers, we are simultaneously assessing, evaluating, identifying, judging, observing, planning, creating, and reflecting, to ensure that our curricular program accommodates all of our individual needs, all of the varying levels of development, all of our varying interests and learning styles, all the required curriculum, and a balanced curricular program. And, good teaching tells us that we must accomplish this through daily routines and known expectations that provide structure for the children, yet remain open-ended and flexible for individualization of content.

The daily curriculum must include a shared reading activity, reading and writing workshop, a teacher read-aloud, independent reading opportunities, a variety of print, and an inquiry-based content study. It must allow for whole-class, small-group and one-to-one instruction with flexible groupings. This must all take place in a classroom environment that is supportive of and nurturing for every child.

We know that the more the children feel safe and cared for, the more they are prepared to learn. The social community also becomes a curriculum consideration in our classroom. It is our job to create a classroom atmosphere that invites learning. It needs to be trusting, inviting, and homey. It must allow for, encourage, nurture, and support the following: classroom community, autonomy, effort, ownership, caring, practice, growth, democracy, honesty, acceptance, respect, value, risk taking, literacy, personal responsibility, success, and self-worth.

In this section we are going to look at some of the actual things that we can do and implement in the classroom that allow us the structure, flexibility, and accountability that we need to be successful with our program.

When we have finished reading this chapter we will have

- completed our classroom environment
- completed writing our yearlong integrated theme
- added all of the components necessary for a balanced yearlong integrated curriculum and literacy program
- integrated all content
- prepared for individualization
- prepared for ongoing assessment
- determined how we will teach each content area
- determined how we will evaluate and establish grades for each content area.

Sustain Ongoing Assessment and Growth

Kidwatching (Goodman and Owocki 2002)

Two kindergarteners, Jenny, an ESOL student, and Romaro, were sitting at their seats working on their morning journals. Romaro was trying to figure out how to spell *February*. As I walked by, I heard Jenny say to Ramaro, "Well, you can turn around and look at the word on the board, you can use your ear spelling, or you can close your eyes and read it in your mind."

Jenny is from Laos. She has been with us in the classroom for only six months. I am always concerned about whether she, and my other children, are receiving an adequate amount of individual instruction. I relaxed a little after overhearing that conversation.

From their talk, I learned that Jenny is using strategies. Not only is she using strategies, but she is aware enough of her own literacy processes to verbalize and share them with a classmate. Jenny knows ways to deconstruct and make sense of print; that is our ultimate goal of instruction. I am comfortable in continuing the pace, frequency, and types of instruction I have been using with Jenny. I know I will need to pay attention to some of her specific knowledge, such as letter recognition or phonemic awareness. These are highly tested areas and Jenny will need to perform well on these tested formats in order to show others the knowledge that she has and employs.

Jenny is a risk taker. She continues to show growth in her schoolwork, and she verbalizes strategies for spelling unknown words. For real-life literacy purposes, I think Jenny will be just fine.

And let's not forget Romaro. Romaro has just shown me what he needs from me. I now have a clearer picture of where he is in his development, and where we need to go.

Now, let's look at a scenario between two other students, Lauren and Logan.

Lauren and Logan are coleaders of their inquiry group. The class was in the midst of preparing things for a final presentation and I overheard Logan tell Lauren not to "worry about it" because he already took care of everything and it was fine. He handed Lauren a piece of notebook paper with some writing on it and walked away. As I watched from my position as a literature discussion group member, I saw Lauren look at the paper for a few minutes, put it down, and cross the room to Logan. In her hand was a stack of index cards. She sat down, and after a brief discussion, he pulled out a piece of paper and they begin to work together on something.

Logan is a student in the gifted program. He is a very athletic class leader who bursts with confidence and machismo. Lauren is rather meek and unassuming. There obviously appeared to be a conflict and I was curious to see what was happening. I was also wondering how Lauren would handle a situation of confrontation independently. When our literature group broke up, I went over to Lauren, who was now working independently. I asked her what was up, what was she working on. She simply informed me that Logan tried to take over the group but the work he did didn't even make sense, so she straightened it out. No big deal. Lauren, too, will be just fine.

Every observable behavior becomes an anecdotal record. These moments document successful literacy behaviors that can never be put into benchmarks or numbers. They complete the total picture of the child. We can now feel and see the child's voice. They become alive to us. Without our observations, our children will be represented solely by numbers on a page. They deserve a face. Kidwatching is our way of identifying ZPDs—and maintaining a total picture of the child.

Establishing Grades

Establishing concrete grades in these areas is not difficult. I have learned to simplify matters throughout the years. First, I establish with my children and parents that I thoroughly understand that what I am observing is but the tip of the iceberg. It is not a direct reflection of the child's ability. I have no way of knowing the problem solving and thinking that is going on in the heads of my children unless they tell me. If they are not standing in front of me, I can only assess what I see, not what I think to be true. I know that a grade is only a measure of that child's performance on that material at that given place and time. Our program has many opportunities for the children to show their literacies and strengths and it is my job to see that that occurs. As long as there are grades, I must establish this trust and understanding to maintain the integrity of my program.

Having said that, I am accountable for stating to the best of my ability what that performance looks like at a specific point in time. If somebody from the state department of education came in and had to grade a paper or a project, what grade would it be? What does an A look like? What does a C look like? In grading all nonstandardized materials, I individualize the grade back to the child who created the work. I know Lauren's work, I know Romaro's work, and I know Logan's work. I know everybody's work and what we have been working on up to this point. I know what is excellent, good, and poor effort for every child in my class. Based on this, here is how I assign letter grades:

A: If Lauren's assignment is absolutely, without a doubt great for Lauren, and she followed all directions and criteria, she will receive an A.

B: If Lauren's assignment is really well done for Lauren, and she followed all directions and criteria, she will receive a B.

C: If Lauren's assignment is average for Lauren, and she followed all directions and criteria, she will receive a C.

D: If Lauren's assignment is below average for Lauren, even if she followed most of the directions and criteria, she will receive a D.

F: If Lauren didn't do the assignment, or her work shows little effort, respect, concern, or personal responsibility, she will receive an F.

Numerical Grades

When I was teaching in Arizona, we gave numerical grades instead of letter grades. Let's see how this transfers by looking at one of Lauren's "A" assignments.

Lauren has an A on her latest project. It is excellent for Lauren. But how excellent is it? There are usually two different grading skills in the elementary school depending on where you live. In some areas, an A = 90 to 100. In other areas, an A = 94 to 100. Lauren lived in Arizona, where the grading scale is A = 90 to 100. I am going to take that A and break it up into even smaller sections.

1. Looking at Lauren's paper, does she have a high A?
   • Is her paper just about perfect paper? If so, she would probably score a 97, 98, 99, or 100.

2. Looking at Lauren's paper, is it a nice solid A?
   - Are there just a couple of little things that could be fixed or improved, but I am still so proud of this work? If so, she would probably score a 93, 94, 95, or 96.
3. Looking at Lauren's paper, how strong is that A?
   - Did she just go over the top of producing *good* work and is on her way to trying more things? If so, she would probably score a 90, 91, or 92.

Establishing numerical equivalents for high, middle, and low letter grades makes assessing and accounting for my grades much easier.

Once we have our first set of grades for all content areas, we can then use these grades as a determination of growth or progress over time, rather than as a statement of students' exact literacy ability.

Develop a Balanced, Individualized Academic Program

Language Arts

It helps to remember that when it comes to our daily lives and the language arts, almost everything we do incorporates or utilizes listening, speaking, reading, or writing. It would be nearly impossible to accomplish anything without applying one of those four domains. We are always using the language arts.

With each new or different exposure to these domains, our schema is broadened and we are better able to assimilate and accommodate new learning in varying situations. We are problem solving appropriate literacy strategies and interactions depending upon our need and setting. We are participating and observing in a working literate environment where our exposure to literacy events and our practices and interactions with print will provide ongoing support and continuance of learning. When all is said and done, the only way to become a better reader is to read; the only way to become a better writer is to write. The same applies to speaking and listening. We must be immersed in and practice all four of these literacies, and with a great deal of simultaneity.

Creating situations that allow for continuous immersion and practice in reading, writing, listening, and speaking for varied purposes is the core of your literacy program. The children need to be reading, and they need to be writing. There are ways to allow for this ownership, progression, practice, choice, and immersion in your literacy program while still allowing you to be accountable, apply some direct instruction, and substantiate a grade.

Sample Schedule

My daily schedule typically uses the same format whether I am teaching primary or intermediate children. All elementary students benefit from the same type of program, activities, literacy experiences, and workshop formats. Only the materials used and concepts taught will change depending upon the grade I'm teaching. Therefore, for me, the only difference between scheduling among the various grades that I teach is accommodating the given lunch and activity/planning times. Otherwise, all else looks the same in an outline format. The following is a rough draft of a typical day:

1. Between first and second bell—The children organize their materials for the day (supplies, homework, books, library books) and get ready for school to begin at the second bell.
2. Second bell—Teacher takes attendance, lunch count. Children work at seats on journals, reading, or morning seatwork. School plays morning announcements.
3. After morning announcements—Children come to carpet for shared reading time (explained later in this chapter), daily or weekly poem, classroom meeting or discussion (as needed), morning share time (Mr. Bear or other student sharing), morning calendar, morning directions, status checks.
4. When students return to seats—Children participate in reading and writing workshop until lunch.
5. After lunch—We have a bathroom break. After that there is a short recess for primary. Then the teacher reads aloud from a novel.
6. After read-aloud—Teacher instructs on content focus. This could be math (anything not integrated) and/or a social studies or science inquiry.
7. After content focus—Clean up, organize, review or discuss day.
8. Dismissal.

When I learn of my activity/planning time and lunch time, I can fine-tune this outline and create approximate time frames that will accommodate my curriculum and school scheduling needs.

Now let's look at some of the elements included in my daily schedule and focus upon what each element entails *to me*, and how they are implemented and applied. Please note, many of the following terms are defined, used, and applied in various ways in educational literature. Their use and definition are highly dependent upon the text or the author. I will be describing each term as I apply it.

Shared Reading

As stated earlier, right after the morning announcements we begin our day with shared reading. To me, this is one of the most important instructional times of our school day. If we can get nothing else accomplished today, we *will* do shared reading. This carpet time is more than just a touchy-feely, community-building, aesthetic enhancement of literature. It is the foundation of my entire language arts program.

Through the modeling of the morning picture book I am able to assess my children's interest, comfort, and participation with print read orally. I am able to observe their listening comprehension and ability to discuss and respond to a story. I can see how my children internalize the print and the types of interactions they choose to have with the text. While Lauren discusses inferences that remind her of when she was little, Karl is just beginning to notice that there are letters in the book that are also in his name. I notice that Jenny is using the illustrations as a strategy for making sense of print. She, in turn, notices the strategies, responses, and interactions of the story generated from her peers. Everybody will bring something different to the task.

Through shared reading we can model various reading strategies and behaviors, and teach all of the skills and story elements found in most structured reading programs. We can model writing strategies that the author used to create such a great story. We can use the book as a springboard to a learning activity in science or as a springboard to a writing activity or as a model for an individual or class book. We are modeling with real materials that are interesting, transferable to new learning situations, and readily available to use and revisit.

The use of picture books and big books in the shared reading experience is a crucial element of your program for establishing a risk-free, aesthetic learning environment. First of all, they are fun. They are beautiful, and everybody loves a good story. Secondly, many of our regular and special needs students will require narrative and expository materials that they can handle independently, and that we can use in small-group or one-to-one situations instructionally. If these are not an accepted, working part of our curriculum then these materials become an embarrassment and stigma when applied in this manner.

Every day, following the picture book, we do our morning poem. The poem allows me to see how my children handle print of another genre—how they discuss poetry and illustrate poetry. Because it's on chart paper and allows for repetition, I can observe who focuses upon the structures and conventions of the print. Who follows along with the text? Who looks at the words? Who has one-to-one correspondence? When we play "What Do We Notice" with the poem, I can observe and assess the strategies the children use and the skills and concrete knowledge they employ. I can model and introduce word families, *daily oral language* activities, colorful language, spelling, the difference between a line and a sentence, dialect, decoding strategies for unknown words, descriptive language, inference, poetry styles, vocabulary, poetry writing, contractions, quotations, compound words, grammar, and phonemic awareness.

Depending on each child's developmental level, interest, and learning place, everybody will have something different to bring to our literacy events, and everybody will be able to take something different away. I will be able to introduce quality literature and poetry, nonchalantly teach language arts skills and strategies, and observe and assess the children's literacies and behaviors in these areas every morning.

Reading Workshop

Reading workshop refers to the times that we intentionally focus upon reading. Whereas shared reading (for me) is always conducted with the whole group, reading workshop is usually conducted in small groups. These small groups will change frequently and be determined by the students' choice of literature for literature discussion groups, targeted assistance for students with similar demonstrated needs, and random heterogeneous groupings. Reading workshop runs simultaneously with writing workshop, described later in this chapter. Therefore, if a child is not working on reading workshop, the child is writing. Reading workshop includes literature discussion groups, skill instruction, and individualized targeted assistance.

Literature Discussion Groups

Literature discussion groups provide for a different type of reading instruction, assessment, and observation. Literature discussion groups allow for the aesthetic purposes of reading. In literature groups the students choose among several books that usually relate to a certain theme. Literature groups focus more on comprehension of text and provide authentic interaction with quality literature that allows each student to internalize and discuss the characters, plot, and setting from her own perspective, experiences, and point of view. Children learn to talk about books, value other people's perspectives, become aware of how print affects people differently, and value their own insights and predictions. Students learn to carry on conversations, practice identifying new words by context, learn to handle a book over a period of time, locate cause-and-effect situations, and problem solve with the main characters.

As teachers, we are modeling, observing, and assessing how the students handle printed material when reading independently. We are providing structured opportunities where the children can choose a literature book and after reading it, respond to it. If the ultimate goal of reading is to be able to read and construct meaning by making sense of print, then we need to give the kids opportunities to read and make sense of print. We need to raise their metacognition by bringing the smart things that they know about reading to the surface. We can model what independent readers do before, during, and after reading. We can examine various ways to respond to a text by making it our own. We can appreciate and enjoy literature. (Remember, if a child chooses not to read, he may as well be a nonreader.)

Through literature discussion we can individualize instruction by offering more choice and range of materials. For example, in the primary grades, if we are studying the moon, then Logan may be reading a very simple book such as *A Child's Goodnight Book* (Brown 1992; low performance). Jenny could be reading *Papa, Please Get Me the Moon* (Clare 1986; medium performance) and Molly could be reading *The Moon* (Gibbons 1997; high performance). In instructional settings these books could be used in addition to our printed material and leveled books that deal with the moon as the subject.

In the intermediate grades, if we are studying character development and reading books with memorable female characters, Karl may be reading *The Secret Life of Deborah Samson* (McGovern 1975; low performance). Lauren may be reading *Charlotte's Web* (White 1952; medium performance), and Teresa may be reading *The True Confessions of Charlotte Doyle* (Avi 1990; high performance).

We can assess our children's comprehension by watching them read, listening to their interpretations of the story, and looking at their visual responses to the text. All of our children can sit together and discuss the same books or like themes, regardless of ability and current knowledge.

It is my job to support any child who wishes to read any book. If Lauren chooses a book that I know will be difficult for her, then I may question her choice. The ability to choose books wisely is a literacy task that we need to become competent with. If Lauren is aware that the text may be difficult but wishes to read it anyway, I probably will not override her decision. I know that I offered books at her independent reading level and interest that she did not want to read. I know that this is the book she is interested in because she says that she wants to work through the book anyway, and I know that she wants to join her classmates who chose the same text.

I also know that motivation, ownership,[*] and acceptance and inclusion of varying reading abilities are a powerful force in learning. Therefore, I am very pleased that literacy is important to Lauren and that she wants to see herself as a

---

[*]When a person has choice over material and expression, she tends to take more responsibility and interest in that material. It's hers; she chose it. She is therefore more dedicated and involved in the project.

reader and be in the same group with her new best friend. She is willing to apply the effort and perseverance, which means she will be open to advances and suggestions toward help.

Remember, this is just one aspect of our literacy program. I know that Lauren is also immersed in other real-life experiences with print at her instructional level, as well as continuous test-taking and skill instruction that is needed in other literacy arenas. As Lauren works through the book and joins her literature group, she will be able to see how the other children understood the story, and through their discussions she will have additional support for her reading, as well as modeling literature group procedures and ways to respond to print.

She will be writing her literature responses into her reading journal (described later in this chapter), which means I know she will be focusing very heavily on the graphophonics of the text as she copies some of the words, sentences, and title into her journal. During independent reading times Lauren will be able to sit with her literature book and buddy read with some of her friends in the same group. I can also use her literature book for some of our individual one-on-one focus work.

IMPLEMENTING LITERATURE GROUPS: PRIMARY GRADES In the primary grades, the literature discussion groups revolve around selected picture books rather than novels. The books are generally carried over a one-week period and the children respond differently to the same text each day. First, we do a picture walk, which means going through the book and looking at the pictures to see what is happening on each page. A picture walk gives value to prereading experiences that most emergent readers utilize and reinforces that looking at the illustrations is a sound reading strategy and not cheating. Then we read and discuss the book. Next, we may work on phonemic awareness skills and look at all the words that have the long *e* sound but are spelled with -*y* and not by the letters -*ee*. Some days we may read and draw our favorite page, solve words in context, find words that rhyme, act out the book, retell the story, create puppets, or anything related to the text that the children choose to discuss, enhance upon, and/or need to be reinforced. Primary literature groups meet daily.

IMPLEMENTING LITERATURE GROUPS: INTERMEDIATE GRADES To implement literature groups in the intermediate grades, I begin by selecting four or five novels that have a common theme. I will usually have five to ten copies of each novel selected. If we are studying colonization, then my novels will be focused upon Colonial story lines and/or take place during Colonial times. Each book will have something different or reinforcing to add about the Colonial time period. Reference materials such as maps, encyclopedias, picture books, poetry, biographies, time lines, library books, websites, and artifacts will be made available to the students throughout the literature study.

I will begin each new literature study by giving a book talk about each book. I will include author information as well as subject line and readability suggestions (has a lot of dialect, jargon, easy vocabulary, difficult syntax or sentence structure, etc.). I then request that the children write down their first three book choices. (See Literature Sets Ballot in Appendix C.) I will accommodate a student's first choice as much as possible. The class then becomes divided for literature groups dependent upon the students' various book choices. Therefore, these groupings have an opportunity to change with every new literature group study.

After the books are chosen, I disperse them to each student. During our very first literature meeting, the students will receive their novel inside a gallon-size zippered plastic bag. The bag will also contain a small package of stickie notes, a spiral-bound three-ring notebook (one subject), and a reading contract. The stickie notes are for the students to mark places of difficulty, vocabulary to look at, and/or places they want to share and discuss with their group. The spiral notebook is for their reading journal. After each reading the students are required to record their thoughts in their spiral notebook. I provide each student with an open-ended list of reading responses that he may use if he cannot decide upon one of his own. A sampling of these reading responses can be found in Appendix C (see the Reading Journal Assignment).

The reading contract is a document that informs the reading groups of the title of their book and their required reading/pacing schedule. Reading groups meet on Mondays, Wednesdays, and Fridays. Each member of the group is required to read the selected pages for each given day and respond in her reading journal. When the group meets, they sit in a circle and discuss the reading for that day. They may read from their reading journal or just refer to it. Each member is required to be an active participant and listener. The students, parents, and teacher sign the reading contract. Because most novels are carried over a three-week period, every student knows his reading assignment in advance. This is particularly helpful for students who may miss school because of illness or vacations. The contract is also documentation of what each student agrees to accomplish and read. (See Figure 2–1 and Appendix C.)

At the completion of each novel, the students each create a reading project that represents an aspect of the book to share with their group. Reading projects can take on any form or design. Some students have baked an item prominent in the text; dressed liked a character; written a poem; drawn a picture; and created maps, calendars, time lines, magazines, musical scores, videos, models, research reports, graphs, alternate endings, author studies, and so on.

Literature Group Contracts

Note: Literature discussion groups meet on Mondays, Wednesdays, and Fridays. The contract below reflects the pages to be read for that day's discussion. After reading, you are responsible for responding to the book (see your journal response handout) and sharing in group.

Between the dates of <u>October 18th</u> and <u>November 3rd</u>, I agree to read the book entitled <u>Roll of Thunder, Hear My Cry</u>. I will pace myself according to the contract below.

Student's Signature _____

Parent's Signature _____

Teacher's Signature <u>Dr. Coughlin</u>

MONDAY		WEDNESDAY		FRIDAY			
18th p. vii – p.22 chap. 1	19th TUESDAY	20th p. 23 – 51 chap. 2 & 3	21 THURSDAY	22nd p. 52-76 chap 4		23 SATURDAY	24 SUNDAY
25th p. 77 – 105 chap. 5 & 6	26 TUESDAY	27th p. 106 – 129 chap. 7	28 THURSDAY	29th p. 130 – 147 chap. 8		30 SATURDAY	31 SUNDAY
Nov. 1st p. 148 – 183 chap. 9 & 10	2nd TUESDAY	3rd Finish Books LOGS DUE	4th THURSDAY	5th Projects Due Book Test		6 SATURDAY	7 SUNDAY
	TUESDAY		THURSDAY			SATURDAY	SUNDAY

Figure 2–1. Reading contract

The students then take some type of open-ended exam on their book. I have asked students to complete the following tasks:

- Draw a picture of the setting and cite five sentences from the book that tell how the setting looked.
- Create a treasure box for a character in the book. What are five things the character would put in it and why?
- Write about which character you would like for a best friend; use examples from the book to show why.
- Create a story map.
- Sequence events by retelling or acting out the story.
- Compare and contrast two characters using a Venn diagram.

LITERATURE GROUP GRADES The literature discussion groups allow us to observe the children's interactions with real print. In the intermediate grades we are able to substantiate and document a minimum of four numerical or letter grades every three weeks for every book read and discussed. For example, Lauren will receive one grade for each of the following:

1. reading her book according to her contract, following all procedures, journaling in her response log after reading, sharing her responses in the group, participating in the group, and listening and sharing appropriately with her peers
2. her journal responses at the end of the book when the journals are collected
3. the reading project she created and shared at the end of the book
4. her performance on the open-ended book test.

In the primary grades I am concerned about documenting and observing reading growth over time rather than assigning a specific grade. This includes knowing each of my students' current reading ability with various books and tests as well as knowing the developmental progression of literacies and what learning looks like in the classroom.

Skills Through Literature

When using literature for specific skill instruction as well as aesthetic purposes, we should never mix real reading pleasure with our focused skill work. Always, we appreciate the story and discuss the book. Then, we revisit the book later for a different purpose: focused skill instruction based upon some demonstrated individual or group need.

It is very important to establish in your children's minds that skill work is not reading, and reading is not skill work. Always separate the two with the children. We read the story for pleasure first and foremost. This maintains the integrity of *what reading is*, and by having the story read ahead of time, everybody has created a schema (related the story to past experiences and background knowledge) and is familiar with the text. If we choose to use the book in a strategic way, we simply revisit it. We are revisiting the text for a different purpose: to demystify the book and figure out strategies for troublesome areas or to look at the text as the product of a writer, deconstructing the print to see what the author did to make the book so good and create meaning for the reader. The literature groups are why we read: to appreciate books. The skill sessions are to help us read. A very simple demarcation is all that is necessary. It may sound something like this:

> Isn't that a great story? I like it too. Let's look at it again for a minute. I just want to show you something I noticed while I was reading. Do you see over here on this page where he swallows the ocean? The author used the word *gulped*. (Write *gulped* on the white board.) What does this word mean? How do we know? What would or could we do if we came to this word in our reading and we didn't know what it said? How do we solve unknown words? Did the illustrator give us any clues? Look at the letters in the word. It begins with a *g*. What sound could this letter make? Look at the ending, *-ed*. Can we break the word down into parts that we know?

And so on.

Individualized, Targeted Reading

Guided reading, instructional reading, small-group instruction, reading recovery procedures, individual one-on-one focus work . . . I do not know what to call the more direct instructional times in our reading program. To say that this is my instructional reading time seems to negate the fact that everything we do is for the purposes of instruction and increasing our strategies and schemata. So, as far as I am concerned, anytime that I am working with a student for the purposes of progressing her learning *and* my instruction is based on my knowledge of literacy processes and her ZPD, then I am teaching reading.

When I am working with children individually or in a small group, it is because I have identified a specific area of need that we are going to focus on and practice. This is the time when I have more control over the materials and the activities we do. I choose the books we use based upon the student's independent reading approximations. The purpose of these instructional times is to work on needs specifically demonstrated by the student. My instruction appears more direct at these times. In these learning situations we will be reading books, writing stories, working on skills and strategies in the context of the book or written story, and employing such things as cut-up sentences, word walls, word sorts, magnetic letters, language experience activities, graphic organizers, book writing, and specific test-taking skills. During this time I will also administer assessments with running records and miscue analysis as needed. On the days we don't have literature groups I know I will work with some of the children individually. In addition, by knowing where my children are in their learning, everything—including reading a sign on the way to lunch—becomes a guided reading moment.

Additional Reading and Practice Throughout the Day

Test-taking Strategies

In the intermediate grades we occasionally spend some time (about ten minutes or so before shared reading) at our seats working on test-taking skills. Typically, I take all of the assessments and workbook skill pages from the adopted reading series and put them on transparencies. I use the reading series as a primary source because it has exact representations of the assessments the children will need to accomplish independently. These assessments also utilize the same bubbling format as our standardized tests. The children read the transparency and secure their answers in their heads. When everybody has had an appropriate amount of time to read and choose his answers, we discuss the transparency together as a class. We deconstruct the assessment. First, we respond to the questions and establish the correct answers. Then we figure out how each answer was solved and clear up any misconceptions that arise along the way.

Independent, Free-choice Reading

There are many opportunities for independent, free-choice reading. The classroom library supports and respects all kinds of print as legitimate reading materials. Remember, the goal is to get children reading independently so they can and will practice on their own, thus increasing their own literacy without the need for constant adult support. Stopping a child from reading the material she chose and is engaged in simply because I do not deem it educational enough is not only disrespectful but not common sense. Reading a comic book or baseball cards can accomplish my goals just as well, if not better, than the novel I would have chosen for the child. However, this time period is called *independent reading*. If I do not want, trust, or allow my children to choose school-appropriate materials, then I need to call this reading time something else. Observing children and their choices of reading materials is in itself an ongoing assessment of their individual reading behaviors, levels, attitudes, and confidence.

I can observe children's reading behaviors, the way that they approach and feel about print, by watching them during independent reading. Some children request to have additional reading time. This informs me that the child likes to read and chooses to read as a free-time activity. Because children like to spend time at what they are good at, I would also assume that this was a competent or a confident reader who enjoys books and magazines. The motivation and interest are there. This is a child that will continue to grow in her learning. I am not as concerned about the child who chooses to read, even if that child is below grade level. I know I can teach him because he will let me.

I am more concerned about the children who avoid reading, whether they are considered competent (which usually means that they are reading materials deemed to be on grade level) or not. There are some children who simply avoid reading during this independent time. These children have made an art out of looking busy and involved. However, consistent observation shows that this type of student wanders a lot, uses the bathroom, has difficulty selecting a text she wants to read, returns to and from the bookcase numerous times, asks to help the teacher or do an errand, visits with her peers, sits with a friend who has a book, continually reads the same book, reads books that are extremely easy for her, and/ or chooses to read materials that contain more pictures than story, such as hidden picture books, encyclopedias, nature magazines, picture dictionaries, pop-up books, photo albums, ABC books, simple counting books, and class-made books.

This child tells me that it is going to take more direct instruction, creativity, and guidance on my part in order to continuously observe and sustain growth in reading ability and strategies. This child does not enjoy reading and therefore will not practice the reading of text unless watched and monitored. The child may be totally competent and reading on grade level; however, interest, attitude, and motivation prevail in the long run. The only way to become a better reader is to read. So, we can only teach a child as much as he allows us to.

In addition to silent reading, whisper reading, and buddy reading, independent reading is built into other structures of our classroom program. In the younger grades, my children maintain what we refer to as envelope books.

Envelope Books
At the beginning of the school year, each child receives a giant manila envelope to decorate. Taped to the front of the envelope is a letter of explanation. Inside the envelope is a reading log that accommodates approximately twenty books (all envelope book forms are located in Appendix C). The log states the date and the title of the book read. The child's parent then notes whether the book was a Goldilocks book (a term I borrow from Dr. Karri Williams, one of my reading professors) or not. I want to keep the children progressing with books that are *just right*. When the children choose a book to read, they put it in their envelope and bring it home. Depending on the child and the book chosen, I or another classmate may read that book with the child before it goes in the envelope. If it is a book that requires some concentration, such as a new text, then it is important

to read it first with the child so she has a structure that can help her practice, especially if you know there is little support at home.

The children read and practice their envelope books. After practicing, they read the book to either the class or me. When the book is successfully read, they can choose a sticker to put on their envelope, and then choose another book. I like my children to switch their envelope books at least once a week.

Through envelope books I can observe my children's book choices, monitor their reading of independent choices, notice their ability to handle various texts, give the children opportunities to choose and practice instructional reading in an independent, risk-free setting, and make sure they have something to read in the house that they enjoy.

Another way I encourage and provide opportunities for independent reading is with Mr. Bear.

Mr. Bear

Mr. Bear is a stuffed bear that goes home with the helper of the day. I usually use a Paddington Bear (Bond 1968) because he is a literary character and he comes with a tag asking the "bearer" to please take care of him. When we were studying the oceans the class also wanted a Mr. Whale. The helper of the day then got to choose whether she would take home Mr. Bear or Mr. Whale as her evening companion. Winnie the Pooh was used when we studied The 100 Acre Woods, and when we studied Zuckerman's Farm, we used barnyard animals instead of bears.

Mr. Bear goes home with the helper of the day inside his own Mr. Bear backpack. Inside the backpack with Mr. Bear is a folder that contains the child's share sheet for the next day of school (see Mr. Bear form in Appendix C). The child brings Mr. Bear home and sometime that evening introduces him to his family and reads him a story. After reading, the child records the date and title of the book on his share sheet. They (Mr. Bear and the child) then write and/or draw about their favorite part. The child shares his share sheet with the class the following day. The share sheets are kept in our Mr. Bear three-ring notebook to read and look at during independent reading times.

Daily Calendar Time and Language Arts

For the primary children, there is a great deal of language arts learning and teaching that can take place during our math calendar time. Our math calendar time takes place in a whole-group setting near the math calendar bulletin board area. Pulling from calendar activities employed from *Mathematics Their Way* (Baratta-Lorton 1995) and various mathematics textbooks, I expose children to the same print and procedures daily through the context of math. This repetition of print and repeated modeling of strategies provides a scaffold for the emergent reader and opportunities to explore for the independent reader.

Figure 2-2. Reading area and Mr. Bear

Figure 2-3. Daily calendar and helper calendar

While doing the calendar we can individualize depending upon the task and the child. For example, if Tony is making today's date (the 12th) out of coins, he may choose to make it with twelve pennies. Shelby may see that she can make twelve with a dime and two pennies, and Sarah may notice that she can trade Shelby's dime for two nickels. Rashan may notice that the number 12 has a 2 in it; and Jenny may notice that the word *penny* starts with a *p*. These are all things that identify the children's zones of proximal development.

The math calendar and daily classroom routines provide constant practice and interaction with print. By doing the morning calendar, we are reinforcing math skills while practicing daily with

1. repeated, predictable text
2. identifying, reading, and making meaning out of words and print in our environment for functional purposes
3. applying reading strategies and skills in context
4. increasing vocabulary, use, and sight word comprehension of math-related language
5. connecting and noticing patterns of language
6. interpreting words into number sentences and number sentences into words
7. creating real-life word problems
8. discussing and making sense of our world through different forms of print
9. authentic print.

With the repeated exposure my children have to printed materials, I am constantly able to evaluate and document reading objectives and goals that I consider to be signs of a strong reader. See the Reading Objectives and Goals Checklist in Appendix C for a sampling of what I can learn about my readers.

Writing Workshop

In writing workshop, I have an opportunity to observe my children's writing behaviors and performance from brainstorming to finished product, July to June (I teach at a year-round school). I can see their growth, their practices and revisions, their choices, their problem solving, their spellings, their conventions of print,* their approximate level of development, and where we should go in our

---

Conventions of print is a term used to identify the use of conventional—or correct—spelling. For example, if the child is using *invented spelling* (what I call *ear spelling*), then we can look to see how many conventions are employed in his spelling attempts. How many words does the child spell correctly? How conventional is he at this stage in his development? Conventions can also refer to correct aspects of print demonstrated in the student's writing, such as spaces, capitalization, punctuation, indenting, and so on.

instruction. Their writing workshop notebook is also used as data and record-keeping material for report cards and conferences, as well as writing IEPs (Individualized Education Plans, used with special needs students). See the Writing Workshop Objectives and Goals Checklist in Appendix C for a sampling of what can be learned from a student's writing workshop notebook.

How Writing Workshop Is Implemented

At the beginning of the year, each child receives a large three-ring binder and notebook paper. If the children are younger, in grades K and 1, I will offer them lined paper for their notebooks, but usually we begin on three-hole-punched plain white copy paper. This allows the children the freedom to develop their small-motor coordination for letter writing and drawing without the burden or panic of having to get the words correctly spaced on the lines. Blank paper also allows for the children to create and work at their developmental level: words, labeled pictures, sentences, stories, drawings, strings of letters.

By looking at my daily schedule, you can see that writing workshop runs simultaneously with reading workshop. We transition from morning calendar to our scheduled reading and writing workshop time. When we are finished with our morning calendar, I will take a weekly Writing Workshop Status Checklist (see Appendix C for all writing workshop forms), which I keep on a clipboard in my reading area. Using my status checklist, I will run down our class roster and each student will tell me what he plans to work on in writing workshop that day. This works as a verbal contract between the student and myself. Children may say they will be working on a new story, revising, editing, creating a card, writing a letter or a poem, creating a poster, brainstorming, researching a writing topic, publishing, and so on.

The children are then dismissed to gather their writing workshop notebooks and proceed on their agreed-upon tasks. We write every day. The following are the rules of writing workshop:

1. Write daily.
2. Date every paper.
3. Throw nothing out.
4. Don't erase.

Drafts of writing are considered as important as the finished project. I must see the processes my children go through in writing in order to determine their strengths, weaknesses, and development and tailor my interactions and lessons to their demonstrated needs.

Writing workshop is almost always free-choice writing. Depending upon the need, we may work on class books or research projects to finalize them, but generally, it is the choice of the author. By allowing the children to generate and create their own print, we are supporting them as authors in the context of authentic writing. The individual creations, the open-ended nature, and the autonomy of writing workshop allow for individual growth. It allows me to individualize writing lessons and adjust expectations for each child.

While the children write, I help edit, gather materials for publishing, conference with students, and help generate ideas. On Mondays, Wednesdays, and Fridays, the students will also participate in reading workshop. When it's time for a literature group (and/or skills group) to meet, the children leave their writing and join their reading group on the carpet. When the reading discussion is completed, the children return to their writing and a new group joins me. Writing workshop ends with a ten-minute sharing of what we have written and worked on that day.

Writing workshop is but one aspect of our writing curriculum. To support ongoing writing experiences throughout the day, we engage in a variety of activities.

We maintain two or three author bags in the classroom for checkout. These bags may go home with students who wish to create in the evenings. The bags contain supplies typically desired of any author and illustrator: paper, watercolors, pencils, crayons, scissors, glue, stapler, and tape. If the student is younger, the bag may also contain lists of words that the child desires to use, word families, or words related to our theme.

Journals are used at different times for various intents. Sometimes I will employ morning journals. Morning journals are used for free responses and sharing with peers. The children write down something they would like to share or tell their classmates. The children then share their morning journals with their table after morning announcements. I've used math journals for creating our own story problems and science journals for nature explorations, logs, and observations. The younger children also focus on writing and producing text in a more expository genre. The children maintain a science observation log. We examine a chosen object and identify its basic attributes of size, shape, color, texture, and weight. Each week we record our observations on a log sheet and keep them in our folder. Through our weekly science observations, the children work through the scientific processes and employ literacy strategies for different authentic purposes.

In the domain of language arts, the science observation allows us to

1. read repeated, predictable text
2. identify, read, and make meaning out of words and print in our environment for functional purposes

3. apply reading strategies and skills in context
4. increase vocabulary, use, and sight word comprehension of science-related language
5. connect and notice patterns of language
6. interpret senses of sight, sound, smell, touch, and taste into words
7. discuss and make sense of our world through different forms of print (such as maps, graphs, charts, encyclopedias, printed directions, and storybooks).

This science log now also becomes data for informing me of the child's ZPD and showing development over time. We also write in dialogue journals, which are used as a communication between the student and me and/or the parents and me; reading response journals, which students use to record thoughts after literature reading; and diaries, a place where students can write their most personal thoughts and know they won't be viewed or read by anybody but them. These are all authentic ways to use various forms of print for different functions.

Additionally, posting notes and letters from the children on the walls, writing messages to the students, designing class stationery, creating class books, establishing pen pals, creating research projects, writing a class newspaper, maintaining a class mailbox, writing invitations to parents to attend school events, creating posters for school events, making greeting cards for the children's family or school staff, and writing thank-you notes to classroom guests and visitors are all authentic ways to incorporate writing into our daily routine.

Language Arts and Content-Area Inquiry Projects

Besides helping children acquire specific knowledge, inquiry-based content study allows many opportunities for immersion, exploration, and practice in expository writing and reading. The children will now be reading and creating print for a different purpose. They will need to locate information and synthesize it into a presentational form. Lauren may choose to outline her presentation and present it in the form of a speech. Karl may use overheads and draw most of his representations. Molly may choose to act out her inquiry through music, art, and drama.

While each child goes through similar literacy acts of retrieving and synthesizing information from various resources, their products are each quite individual and their own. They are physical representations of the child's authentic developmental zone. How creative is the project? How creatively can the student manipulate and use print? What are the child's effort and attitude like? Is this her best work?

Remember, our job is one of coach and supporter. We are the ones who must be proactive and ask questions of our children. We cannot just assign an inquiry project and then wait for the due dates. We must help our children learn how to organize and plan long-term projects and break these goals into smaller, manageable objectives. I need to show Lauren various ways to organize her materials and keep notes. Karl needs to see some ways to organize charts and graphics. Molly wants to work on taking her notes and making them look like something she wants to share and say artistically. My job is to continually circulate and ask my students, "How can I help you?" Besides absorbing content knowledge, the student

- outlines, graphs, and webs
- reads for a specific purpose
- locates and uses reference materials
- organizes notes and creates a cohesive text
- employs all stages of the writing process interactively as needed
- brings a writing piece to completion in published form
- creates a written and visual project from materials learned
- presents the project to the class
- employs listening and public-speaking skills
- employs skimming and scanning strategies
- takes responsibility for his own learning.

All inquiry projects and tests receive two grades. One grade is for the content of the paper. How well did the child respond to her inquiry? How accurate and thorough is it? Is this the child's best work? A second grade is received for the conventions of the paper (the accuracy of spelling, spacing, punctuation, paragraphs, quotations, and grammar). How well did the child bring this piece to final form? The latter grade will be included with the student's writing scores from writing workshop and other written graded assignments. It is very likely to see a student receive a grade of A/D or D/A. In the first case, the child presented me with a great project, but the mechanics were not corrected. The paper it is written on is half ripped out of a notebook with smudges all over it. It's not in neat handwriting, sentences are not capitalized consistently, and there are common spelling errors. I have no other drafts accompanying this paper as required. Not an acceptable finished piece of writing.

In the second case, the student turned in a beautiful paper. Every single thing is perfect—except he didn't answer the question.

Math

Most of my directed teaching of math is conducted with the whole group on the carpet. I use the adopted math textbook for any of the worksheet-type math practice and assessments that we may employ. Typically, after looking at all of the requirements, and integrating as best I can, I determine what will need to be taught more directly. I will then jump around the textbooks as needed. However, most of the time our math is incorporated into some ongoing project, like walking the Appalachian Trail or planning our garden.

The younger children will spend a great deal of time exploring with the manipulatives (both directed and independently) and creating their own understandings of numeracy, place value, estimation, measuring, volume, and patterns. Daily math procedures of voting for lunch, counting out pencils and snack materials, creating word problems out of our morning attendance, graphing preferences, creating Venn diagrams, searching for patterns, and participating in daily calendar activities are structures that allow for ongoing interaction, involvement, individualization, observation, and assessment of growth over time. These open-ended activities lead to familiarity, repetition, and routine for the children. These structures encourage experimentation, autonomy, and problem solving at the child's developmental level. The children can participate at any level.

We can individualize instruction further by seeking out simple ways to help our children become independent. For example, by using graph paper instead of notebook paper for addition and subtraction problems, we can help the children line-up their numerals to keep the integrity of the place values. This helps younger children grasp the concept that maintaining place values is important. It also helps children who have spatial problems keep place values in proper columns.

In another example, Lauren maintained a file box that worked as her memory. One section was devoted to math operations. It contained step-by-step procedures (with examples) of how to do such things as long division, adding and subtracting mixed fractions, and so on. Use of her file box for assessments was written into her IEP as an accommodation strategy. Lauren could do the math required. She just couldn't remember that she knew it. The mere presence of the file box alone gave her control, comfort, ownership, and autonomy.

What can you show your children that will help them continue learning when you are not around to help? What arsenal of supplies or flexibility can you offer them?

Support Immersion in the Classroom Environment

Next, I must attend to the physical environment of my classroom. It must support my philosophy and methods of teaching. The room must accommodate areas for whole-class instruction, small-group work, independent work, cooperative groupings, and autonomous centers or stations.

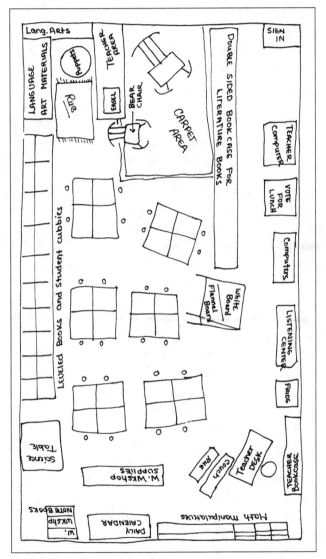

Figure 2–4. Classroom map

The classroom must allow for autonomy and individuality. The children must be able to work creatively at their own progression without constant support from me. I must find time to focus on individual and small-group instruction without constant interruption. I also do not want to give the children any worksheet-type materials so that everybody is doing the same task; it's not individualized and there are more literate ways of keeping the children occupied and engaged so that I can teach.

Therefore, everything in my room must provide a learning opportunity. The children are grouped in sets of four to facilitate cooperative learning, social skills, and the art of conversation and discussion. They are problem solving academically and socially among one another and learning how to discuss and respect the opinions of their peers. And, I know that by talking among themselves, they are increasing their listening comprehension and subsequent reading potential. I like to set my room up so that all of my manipulatives and supplies are readily available for use by the children. This can easily be accomplished by purchasing clear storage tubs and several plastic rolling drawers and bins. When all learning materials are accessible, there is no need to create extra centers or learning experiences for the children. When they are finished with their assigned work, they can attend any area and use any of the available materials and supplies. Therefore, when students are done, they can work with such items as the geoboards or white boards, visit the science table, complete puzzles, play with the Unifix cubes, or simply read and write.

I will need areas for writing supplies, independent reading books, math manipulatives, listening center materials, science inquiry, puppets, art supplies, free time, language art manipulatives, shared reading and whole-class instruction, and seating for twenty-five children split into groups of five. These areas must be created so that they provide availability and structure for both the children and myself.

There needs to be a whole-class area for shared reading, most of the math, comfortable independent reading, class gatherings, and so on. This area must allow for a white board or blackboard, a reading chair, and a carpet. Because most reading groups are conducted here, there should be some space for miscellaneous teacher supplies, checklists, the teacher read-aloud novel, and copies of the books being read in literature groups.

Classroom materials are a key factor in accommodating needs. Varied materials are extremely important for establishing risk taking, comfort, and acceptance. It must be as accepted for a sixth grader to read a big book as a read-aloud as it is for him to read an encyclopedia. The more choice of materials, the more varied the needs, interests, experimentation, and developmental levels I can accommodate.

The writing area needs to contain writing supplies, publishing materials, writing ideas, and address books. There needs to be an area to store all of the writing workshop notebooks throughout the year, and folders or portfolios for finished pieces of oversized, bulky work that is still in progress.

The art area needs to contain a plethora of varied craft and supply items.

The science area needs to provide space for us to do our weekly science observations and establish a discovery zone where found treasures such as plants, seeds, nests, mold, bugs, magnets, and egg shells are kept and explored. Science-related books are great to keep here, as well as some magnifying glasses, a scale, some lab coats, measuring tape, and some clipboards.

The math area needs to accommodate various math-related materials. The children should be able to pull out the materials they wish to work with as needed. This means that I must have an area that contains such items as games, manipulatives, calculators, and so on.

(See Appendix C for a more complete listing of suggested area materials and supplies.)

Conclusion

It's easy to see how the last three criteria overlap, enhance, and support one another in both theory and application. Additionally, they each contribute to the success, failure, and future of our students.

We have just completed our most taxing and important work: establishing our curriculum and environment to support and meet individual needs and standards. It's time for chocolate and the rest of the day off!

3

Setting Up Your Classroom

Establishing a classroom environment is highly dependent upon

- the physical structure of our room
- the grade we are teaching
- the manner in which we like to teach.

Our objectives are to create a classroom that is

- functional
- aesthetically pleasing
- emotionally supportive
- intellectually stimulating.

Functional

When our rooms are functional we

- expedite the amount of time it takes to write lessons
- spend less time gathering and locating materials
- advance our classroom management by providing less downtime (everything we need is at our fingertips or able to be grabbed quickly)
- provide a constant organizational structure for our students, while modeling the skills of organization, being prepared, and planning ahead.

It is our job to create the teaching areas we desire and require. However, we must work within and around the built-in physical structures and layout of the classroom. Therefore, the first thing we must do is view our new room.

It is a good idea to discuss the school's procedures on entering your classroom during hours the building is closed. You will need a key to the building and to your classroom. You may also need a key to allow you access to a restroom and/or copy machine. The principal and/or school secretary can generally provide you with this information. In some cases you may also need to know how to work the school's alarm system and how to contact the on-campus security guard. You may also wish to find out how your thermostat works and if the air conditioner is working on the weekends or during vacations.

In this chapter we will map out our room, design our room arrangement, and choose our classroom colors.

MATERIALS

- Classroom Planning Sheets (Appendix C: Forms 3a through 3f) or a notepad
- a tape measure (*Note:* Many floor tiles are one foot square. This information may assist in a quick estimation rather than measuring.)
- something to write with
- something to write on, such as a clipboard

Are you ready to begin? Here's our new room:

- cinder blocks, painted beige, chipping to green in some areas; dirt smudges around the lightswitches
- small waist-high cupboards with doors that stretch across the far wall near the sink area
- a door leading into a storage-pod area
- three bulletin boards
- a white board
- a blackboard
- a folding wooden wall that serves as a permanent room divider (western wall)
- furniture piled in the center of the classroom

Activity 1: Sketching the Room

1. Using Form 3a from Appendix C and standing at the front door looking into your classroom, sketch an outline of your new room.

2. When completed, locate, draw, and label the following items on your map:
   - doorways
   - windows
   - bulletin boards
   - blackboards
   - permanent shelving.

Don't worry about proportions or drawing skills. Your objective is to simply create a quick visual representation of your classroom.

Activity 2: Describing Your Classroom Surroundings

1. Look around your classroom again.
   - What materials are the walls made from—cinder block, metal, wood, plastic, cork?
   - What colors are the walls?
   - What color is the sink area?
   - What color is the door?

2. Record this information directly onto your map in the proper location. For example:
   > east wall—beige, cinder block
   > sink area—natural wood, dark
   > file cabinet—light green, metal
   > ceiling—white pressboard/false ceiling tiles

Activity 3: Locating Electrical Outlets, Cables, and Phone Jacks

1. Locate all of the electrical outlets, cables, and phone jacks in the room. Draw them on your map. Note whether the outlets are three-pronged or two-pronged.
2. At some point soon, check with the media or technology specialist to see if there are any outlets in your classroom that are solely reserved for technology. These designated outlets, known as *clean* outlets, are usually easily identified. Typically there are only one or two clean outlets in a room, and they are newer looking and of a different color than the other classroom outlets. Plugging any other electrical device into these clean outlets will interfere with the running of the school equipment and the item you are operating. When known, note the clean outlets on your maps.

3. You now want to determine what outlets in the room are available for your resources that require electricity. You may need outlets for
    - an overhead projector
    - a listening center
    - a tape recorder
    - electric pencil sharpeners
    - an aquarium
    - a microwave
    - computers
    - a television
    - a VCR
    - lamps
    - a telephone
    - some microscopes
    - clocks
    - a cooking area
    - science experiments
    - fans.

When making placement determinations, there are two important factors to consider: convenience and safety.

Convenience
Some electrical resources are utilized more than others. Some resources need to be located in specific areas. When assigning outlets to materials, you may have some priorities based upon your own classroom needs. Make sure you are setting up your room functionally and logically. It's much smarter and easier to spend the time arranging your room logically now than to redo it throughout the year. When assigning resources to outlets, consider all needs:

- Is there an outlet located near the sink or door for easy maintenance of the aquarium?
- Do you have outlets for electric pencil sharpeners in one specific area that could function as a writing center?
- Are there outlets for microscopes in an area that would make a good science center?
- Where will the overhead projector go?
- Are there outlets for tape recorders in a place that would accomodate a listening center?

- Can your computers and other equipment be easily unplugged in case of inclement weather or in preparation for breaks?

TEACHER'S NOTE: This planning is important and can save much aggravation and time if done properly from the beginning. Always keep an easy access to every outlet that is utilized. If your extension cords, cables, and plugs are in an outlet behind a now-too-heavy filing cabinet or a no-longer-moveable shelving unit, then performing simple routines like unplugging or relocating equipment will become frustrating and time-consuming. Do it correctly now. Using outlet strips with their own breaker makes multiple uses and access much easier.

Safety

With regard to safety, you need to ensure that the plugs and extension cords are

- away from water areas
- not interfering with walk or play areas
- not overloading one single outlet.

With safety and function in mind, attempt to determine probable locations for needed electrical items. Do this on your first visit for three reasons:

- You need to estimate how many extension cords, power switches, and prong adapters you will need.
- You need to ensure that you have sufficient outlet resources to accommodate your needs.
- You do not have much choice about the functional placement of electrical items. The electrical items need to be placed first so that you can decorate and design the room around them.

Activity 4: Looking at Wall Space and Mountings

Next, turn your attention to the walls. You've already noted the material and color of the walls on your map. Now you are looking to see what wall space is available for classroom objects. Wall space is often used for

- framed pictures
- signs
- children's class work
- posters
- maps
- projector screens

- a daily calendar area
- clocks
- shelves
- an American flag
- big book holders
- chart holders

- procedures
- agendas
- instructional displays

- center areas
- storage space

1. Look at what you wish to display and where you would like each item to go.
2. Check out the ease and logic of your decision. These resources require various sorts of hanging fixtures. Depending upon the material of the wall, attaching the item could be a very easy task, or a very difficult one. How does the item need to be attached to the wall? What tools or materials will this require? Some materials typically required for hanging resources on classroom wall fixtures are

    - tape
    - Velcro
    - hook screws
    - sticky tape
    - magnets
    - magnetic tape
    - magnetic hooks
    - curtain rods
    - hot glue
    - tacks
    - staples

    - pushpins
    - suction cups
    - screws
    - nails
    - hammer
    - drill
    - Phillips head screwdriver
    - flathead screwdriver
    - concrete anchors
    - molly bolts

3. On your map draw in any determinations of wall attachments made thus far.
4. On Appendix C: Form 3c, record the materials you think you will need to secure each item to the wall. Record the item being attached, the location, and the materials possibly needed.
5. On Appendix C: Form 3b, record notes of placement ideas you are playing with.

Activity 5: Locating and Measuring Classroom Boards

Next, turn your attention to the classroom boards that are permanent wall fixtures. These are bulletin boards, chalkboards, and/or white boards.

1. Locate, sketch, and label all classroom boards onto your maps. Don't worry about exact dimensions or proportions right now. Just roughly draw them in.
2. Now, measure each board to determine its area (height times width). Record this information for each board you drew on your map.
3. Record this information on Form 3d.

Activity 6: Locating and Measuring Windows and Curtains

1. Locate and draw all of the classroom windows onto your map. Don't forget to include any windows that are on doors. Each window will receive two different sets of measurements.
2. First, measure for the window:
   a. Measuring from top to bottom, record the actual height of the window. Log this information as window height = _____ and record this measurement directly onto your map. Example: window height = 24".
   b. Measuring from side to side, record the actual width of the window. Log this information as window width = _____ and record this measurement directly onto your map. Example: window width = 48".
   The window measurements are therefore 24" x 48".
3. Now, take your second set of measurements. This next set is for the purpose of buying or making curtains:
   a. To measure for curtain height, locate where the curtain rod will go, near the top of the window. Start measuring here. Follow the measuring tape straight down until you come to the desired length of the curtain. Log this measurement as curtain height = _____ and record this information on your map. Example: curtain height = 36".
   b. Now, how wide do you want the curtains to extend beyond the windowpanes? This measurement will determine the width of the curtains as well as the length of your curtain rod. Measure the width of the area you wish to cover. Log this information as curtain width = _____. Example: curtain width = 60". Your curtain formula would therefore be: 36" x 60".
   c. Record this information on Form 3d.

Now, let's look at your classroom furniture.

Activity 7: Taking Inventory of Classroom Furniture

Now you are looking to determine the inventory and condition of the classroom furniture provided. You are looking at student seating and teacher furniture.

STUDENT SEATING
- Is the classroom equipped with individual desks, round tables, or trapezoid tables?
- How many will they seat?

- Are they in good condition?
- Are they adjustable?
- How many chairs do you have?
- What color are they?
- Are they adjustable?
- If desks, is there storage space for books and school supplies?
- Do they all have feet? (*Hint:* If you have linoleum floors, you may wish to cut down on the noise made by chair feet. You can cover the bottom of the feet with rubber pads or tennis balls.)

TEACHER FURNITURE

- Is there a computer table in the room?
- Do you have shelves, bookcases, a file cabinet, storage cabinets, closets, or cubbies? Are the shelving units moveable? Are the shelves adjustable?
- Do you have a teacher's desk? A chair? A flag?
- Are there any extra tables or desks to use as centers?

These are all simultaneous observations you make as you glance around the room.

1. Record your notes regarding classroom furniture on Form 3d.
2. Now, look at the cleanliness and visual appeal of the furniture. What furniture needs to be painted, covered with contact paper, covered with a cloth, stenciled, and/or cleaned? Record these notes and observations on Form 3c.

TEACHER'S NOTE: Check with your school custodians to see if any needed furniture can be located in the building. There may be a furniture storage unit or teachers wishing to trade items. Also check with the school secretaries or principal to find out the procedures for requisitioning furniture from the district. Most districts have a warehouse where teachers can go to obtain no longer utilized materials such as tables, desks, bookcases, filing cabinets, and textbooks. Some of these may be in better condition than the furniture in your room.

With these steps behind you, you can turn your attention toward making your room aesthetically pleasing. You will need your map and notes (Forms 3a–3e) to complete the next task.

Aesthetically Pleasing

During the school year we will spend more waking hours in our classrooms than in our homes. To be conducive to teaching and learning, our classrooms need to be a place we like to go—a place that is pleasantly appealing as well as functional. Our classrooms should

- feel safe and secure to develop growth and community
- encourage conversation, interaction, investigation, and participation
- feel warm, homey, and comfortable
- foster learning.

In order to create this tone we must look at this process like decorating a room that is in our home. We want this room to be calming and fluid. By this, I mean nothing is distracting. Not one item or place stands out; instead the room flows from one area into the next. Even a room with a multitude of supplies, materials, and centers can be organized and arranged in a way that is not overstimulating or chaotic in appearance. The best way to save money and time long term is to take the time to set up our classrooms correctly from the onset. Buying materials, supplies, and furniture simply because it's fun, we like it, or for the purposes of just getting started could mean replacing or getting rid of them later if they don't complement our room or instruction. Setting up a classroom is expensive and time-consuming.

If you are a new teacher and starting fresh, it is smart to set up your room correctly from the beginning. This is not a luxury you will have time or additional money for throughout the year. Once you determine your classroom scheme and arrangement, buy only what you need and what matches. Plan carefully and buy wisely. You will be glad you did.

If you are an experienced teacher and already have classroom materials, then take an inventory of those materials and look to see what needs to be supplemented, deleted, and/or replaced. Keep this list with your plan book. Throughout the year refer to this list when money becomes available to purchase needed classroom items. Slowly replace and add items to your classroom that will complement your classroom scheme. Little by little you will transform your room.

One of the most important ways that you can coordinate your room and create a feeling of calmness and order is through color.

Activity 8: Choosing Colors

Choosing the colors for your classroom is an important decision. Before you buy anything new for your classroom environment, you need to first consider the color scheme of your room. You want your room to be color coordinated, much like the rooms in your home. When choosing colors, think about the following questions:

- What specific tone or mood do you wish to create?
- Do you wish to create a theme-related environment?
- Do you want to use your school colors?
- What are your personal color preferences?
- What colors are already established in the room?
- What colors are the accessory materials and resources you already own?

You must choose one main color and two supplemental colors. The main color will be the most evident color in the room. The two supplemental colors will be used to tie in and accessorize remaining materials.

1. Look at your classroom surroundings. Begin with the existing materials and colors that are already in place. What colors are the floors, walls, cabinets, filing cabinets, cubbies, cupboards, and/or curtains (if in place)? Note these observations on Form 3b.
2. If you've taught before, what colors are the storage containers that you own? What about
   - the cubbie baskets?
   - pillows?
   - stacking shelves?
   - book baskets?
   - curtains?
   - carpets?

Look at what you already own or have. Record these materials and color schemes on Form 3b.

3. Now, look at what you have recorded. Using this information, determine a main color for your classroom. Record this on Form 3b. *Note:* When choosing your colors, stop to think about the following:
   a. What colors are most often used for resource supplies in school catalogs? For example, if you plan on using chart holders, which are often blue, green, yellow, or red, will they coordinate or clash with your color scheme? You want to pick colors that are not special shades and are easy to locate in fabric, plastic baskets, construction paper, and resource supplies. This foresight will save you money and aggravation later.

b. What colors do you want in your room to create a certain tone or mood? Color has a great effect on people. Do you want warmer colors of reds and yellows, or cooler colors of greens and blues? What is best for your children and age group?

4. When your main color is decided, choose two colors that can be used to accent and supply your room. Usually these colors are picked up in such items as carpets, curtains, lamps, bulletin board edgings, baskets, and stencils. When you cannot locate something in your main color, coordinate using your secondary colors. Record these colors on Form 3d.

TEACHER'S NOTE: You may wish to check with the school custodians or secretaries to see if there are any plans in the near future to paint, replace tile, or replace carpets in your classroom. If so, see if you can find out what colors the room will be decorated in. This may save you some time and money now.

Activity 9: Setting Up Centers and Content Areas

Note: This activity may be completed at home.

Now you are ready to look at your supplemental, but necessary, areas in the classroom. When you are arranging areas around your permanent fixtures, it's important to take inventory of all the areas and spaces you may wish to include in your setting. These areas could be

- classroom library
- carpeted meeting place
- location for teaching language arts
- location for small-group or one-to-one instruction writing workshop area
- storage area for your small group or one-on-one materials (leveled books, manipulatives, etc.)
- language arts area for play dough letters, magnetic letters, word cards, etc.
- math manipulative area
- listening center
- place for journals
- place for portfolios
- place for lunch boxes
- place for backpacks and supplies
- place for art materials
- easel
- chart stand
- big book holder
- time-out or quiet area

- science table
- file and record-keeping area
- student textbook and workbook area
- puppet area
- puzzle area
- toys and game storage/play area
- block storage/play area
- *Math Their Way* daily calendar and chart area
- place for returned library books
- place to sign in
- place to vote or graph lunch choice
- place for thematic books and hands-on materials
- computer
- dress-up area
- place for your handbooks and professional materials
- place for tools
- place for cleaning supplies
- place for pets
- place for floor mats or carpet squares
- place to return completed work.

Figure 3–1. Carpeted meeting area and language arts area

Figure 3–2. Easels, author chair, meeting place, and a section of classroom library

1. List all of the areas you desire to include in your classroom.
2. Next, make several copies of your room map from Activities 1 through 6 (Form 3a).
3. Now, using your room maps, sketch in approximate locations for your desired areas. You will need to play with this; thus the several copies. You are trying to determine how your floor and wall space can be used most efficiently and unobtrusively.

Think creatively. For example, can books, mats, or lunches be stored in filing cabinets? Record this information on Form 3b.

Once you have a rough idea of various locations in the classroom and have placed them to the best of your knowledge, you need to stand back and assess the following:

*   Are all of the areas included?
*   Are the areas placed so that they leave floor movement, a place to line-up, and clearance around doors and exits?
*   Does the room look too cluttered or overwhelming?

- How do your shelves and areas look? Do they blend? Do they need painting? Do their colors coordinate? Do their contents distract? (Many storage areas can be distracting and catch your eye. They contain various containers, colors, and shapes that don't always blend with your room. In order to create a sense of calmness, order, and flow, curtains can be made to cover classroom shelves, closets, and bookcases.)
- What areas do you still need to provide for shelves or storage?
- Do any of your shelves or bookcases need to be covered?
- Can areas be changed, moved, and utilized without major time or reconstruction to the classroom?
- Is the room pleasing and functional?

Activity 10: Completing Centers

Make a list of all the classroom areas and centers that you need yet cannot totally accommodate in your room at this time. What is it that you need to make each area complete? A table? A bookshelf? Stacking shelves? A storage tub? A curtain?

1. On Form 3c, list each incomplete center area. Right next to it, list the items that are needed for that area to be considered complete.
2. Now, peruse your areas. What furniture or storage area needs work? Does something need painting, cleaning, curtains, new contact paper, or stenciling? On Form 3b, write down the object and what needs to be done to make it classroom-ready.

Activity 11: Making Shelf and Bookcase Curtains

In our homes we conceal the contents of our closets and cupboards. In the classroom we may want to conceal our shelf and storage units. These are areas that tend to look messy and cluttered. They are often filled with materials and supplies that can be distracting and even overstimulating for some children. Covering our storage and supply areas will allow for some privacy of materials while making our rooms appear flowing, less cluttered, and not overwhelming for the children.

Coverings for shelving units can be made easily and attached creatively. The curtain, or cover, can be tailored to your need. I have seen curtains and coverings attached to various cabinets and shelves by way of curtain rods, hot glue guns, wall staplers, tacks, screws with a spring, and Velcro. I have even seen shower curtains used.

Figure 3–3. Overview of classroom with covered storage

We measure for shelving covers in the same manner we measure for curtains. The one thing we need to determine is whether we want one single drape to pull back over the shelf when in use or two separate drapes to slide back.

1. List on Form 3d all of the areas that need covering.
2. Measure the length and width of the opening on each shelving unit.
3. On Form 3d, record the opening and curtain measurements for each shelf.
4. On Form 3d, record the amount of fabric needed.

Activity 12: Adding the Finishing Touches

When your room is complete and set up, look to determine finishing touches that pull the room together and create the look you want. There are two areas of consideration before you start decorating your room:

1. Clutter—Less is better. Too much in the room causes distractions, dust, and lack of space. Students will bounce from one thing to the next like a

child in a toy store. In a cluttered room, some items never get discovered. Unless it is routinely used and needed frequently, store it.

2. Mold, mildew, dust, allergies, and lice—I love carpet and fabric, but before you start decorating with these objects, consider how they will be kept clean (and if they are flame-retardant).

These finishing touches can be accomplished through

- plants
- pictures
- throw rugs
- lamps
- background music
- potpourri
- placemats

- tablecloths
- baskets
- carpets
- stuffed animals
- pillows
- beanbag chairs

1. Make a list on Form 3c of all the items you need to add to your classroom environment. Be complete, including colors and sizes.
2. Also on Form 3c, record your wish list items for future purchase.

Activity 13: Shopping List

Now, it's time to stop. You need to think, brainstorm, plan, imagine, create, make choices, organize, and shop!

1. Sifting through Forms 3a–d, organize, finalize, and revise your thoughts. Complete your tables and make some firm decisions.
2. Go through these final lists and summarize all needed materials on Form 3e.
3. Have fun!

Moving In

Just like moving into a house, moving into a classroom takes some forethought and some time. We need to create a daily plan and a list of materials to bring with us to get started. Allow yourself four to five days to set up your classroom. This time can be lengthened or shortened depending upon the amount of personal teaching materials you have, the condition of your room, and the amount of previous experience you have had doing this.

Materials Needed

- garbage bags
- antibacterial all-purpose cleaner for glass, countertops, tables, etc.
- rubber gloves
- vacuum cleaner
- carpet deodorizer
- a cleaner that removes magic marker, stickers, and contact paper resin
- extension cords
- bleach
- broom
- dustpan
- scissors
- tape
- stapler
- notepad
- pencil
- hammer
- nails
- screwdrivers
- paper towels
- wash buckets
- sponge

Additional Materials I Desire

- cell phone
- Band-Aids
- aspirin
- cooler with soda
- music
- chocolate and other munchies

Day 1: Cleaning the Classroom

Clean the room. Make sure that you attend to the tabletops, desktops, bathrooms, windowsills, windows, mirrors, floors, carpets, filing cabinets, bookcases, storage buckets, desk drawers, cubbies, and other surfaces.

Day 2: Moving and Arranging Large Furniture

Arrange the large furniture items and desks that are in the classroom. Bring in your large furniture items from home. Arrange your classroom furniture according to your floor map design. (*Note:* To save time, while you're waiting to move in, have the furniture already cleaned, painted, and stenciled.) When the room is arranged you can begin setting up the bulk of it.

Day 3: Arranging the Rest of the Room

Today is the day you bring in and arrange everything else:

- files
- books
- resource materials
- classroom supplies
- teaching materials

Today you can set up your story time area, your writing workshop area, your puppet area, your math area, and so on. When you finish, your room is in place and you have only the finishing touches left to tie it all together.

Day 4: Adding the Finishing Touches

Today you add the final decorative touches:

- curtains
- plants
- carpets, rugs
- lamps
- desk and wall pictures
- baskets
- potpourri

Coordinating Your Setting to Your Theme

Once you have your yearly theme, you can go back to your generic classroom setting and tailor the environment to represent, enhance, and support your studied themes.

This is a time of creativity and fun. If you are exhausted—or out of funds—wait. It can always be a work in progress. These are the finishing touches that reinforce your various themes and enable the classroom setting and themes to truly come together. It is the icing on the cake and should be enjoyed.

The first thing you need to do is examine your theme and come up with some symbolic classroom logos, thematic materials, and/or mascots that represent your studies. For example, while focusing on the theme of Zuckerman's Farm, I would want to focus upon barnyard colors and complete my classroom setting to support the feel and look of a barn or farm. Therefore, I would want a country look of straw flowers, metal buckets, wooden crates, stuffed farm animals, plastic crops, hay bales, county fair touches of blue ribbons and crafts, quilted materials, and items to coordinate classroom signs, learning centers, and labels. I would also want to include items specifically related to *Charlotte's Web*, such as a spider web, spider, stuffed pig, barnyard reading area, Templeton the rat, reading trough, and so on.

I would choose to use neutral-colored burlap for all of the bulletin board backgrounds. The trim would be a colored paper twine, unraveled and stapled in a ruffled fashion around the burlap. The fonts for my bulletin boards, signs, and labels would all be coordinated and reflect the nature of my theme. They may be Crate or Western fonts. In some cases, messages and/or titles may be embedded in a hand-drawn web.

The language of the theme would also be reinforced in our daily routines. Instead of the word *Greetings* on my morning procedure chart, I would use the word *Salutations!* Characters would become metaphors for behaviors. For instance, if somebody were messy, greedy, or ate a lot, then she would be a Templeton. Charlotte and Wilbur provide great fodder for character education and discussion throughout the year.

I would also use similar characters or themes to coordinate most of my signs, centers, and labels. By using like materials, characters, colors, and items to maintain a country theme and look, I would be able to coordinate all of my signs. All of my classroom labels would use the same borders, font, and colors. The bulletin boards would be color-coordinated by using the same or similar materials and text styles. While each board would have its own educational purpose, it would still reflect and carry out our country theme within its decor. Desktop signs, cubbie labels, desk nametags, center signs, and class stationery would all carry through with coordinating to the class mascot, colors, and/or borders and font.

Eventually I will want to look at coordinating my curtains, lamps, carpets, placemats, and shelf coverings to match the print, colors, and tone of the theme. The following are activities that you may want to consider when integrating your theme into your environment:

- painting the file cabinets
- painting the walls
- stenciling the walls
- stenciling the furniture
- utilizing storage containers that match your theme for items such as books, manipulatives, magazines, student supplies, desktop centerpieces (These could include crates, buckets, baskets, plastic tubs, porcelain basins, luggage, bathtubs, flowerpots, wagons, wheelbarrows, or anything your creativity suggests.)
- making curtains containing your theme
- developing and creating a class logo
- coordinating your character education and class procedure verbiage around your theme and characters
- coordinating your colors, textures, and prints
- coordinating all bulletin boards, signs, and labels
- decorating your room with photos or items utilized or represented in your theme
- starting a book collection to support your theme
- creating classroom stationery and logos.

Allow your mind to wander and think of the possibilities.

TEACHER'S NOTE: It's easy to get caught in a mindset of buying everything we see that matches our theme. Try not to do this. First, we don't need everything. We won't use everything, we do not have the room for everything, and eventually we'll probably forget we even have it. Then we will start feeling guilty that we aren't using everything we purchased. We'll feel the need to incorporate more simply because "we have it." Inadequacy and panic set in . . . simply because we bought too much.

Secondly, we don't even know this theme is going to work, or be a theme we want to continue to build upon. Don't spend a major amount of money decorating around something you are not sure of yet. Keep it simple. As you go through the year you'll see what you want and what you actually use and could need. Remember, everything is a work in progress; every day is just another rough draft.

When finished, stand back and admire your classroom. Pat yourself on the back, turn off your lights, and go home. You did a good job!

Tomorrow's another day, and there's still a lot of work to do before the children arrive. Chapter 4 will turn our attention to the area of record keeping and classroom management. What do we need to have in order before school starts?

4

Organizing Your Classroom Management System

We will now focus upon readying for the school year from a managerial point of view. Specifically, we will

- identify and create our beginning-of-the-year letters, forms, and lists
- set up our record-keeping system
- create record-keeping forms
- create record-keeping and management materials
- create record-keeping checklists
- set up our student records and files
- organize our yearly assessments
- identify additional materials we need to create, make, or put together
- stock our classroom with needed supplies.

Lists, Letters, and Forms

Depending upon your age group and the manner of your teaching, you may need all or only some of the following items:

- a First Day of School Child Information Form (Appendix C: Form 4a)
- a Parent Information Form (Appendix C: Form 4b)
- a parent letter
- a Class Information Form and Blank Class Roster (Appendix C: Forms 4e and 4f)
- a class supply list for students.

First Day of School Child Information Form

This is a form for the parent or guardian of younger children to complete upon entering the classroom the first day of school—a kindergarten must.

This is necessary because information on the first day of school can often be different from the child's permanent school records and procedures. For example:

- Transportation may vary the first week. Many parents of bus students often drive their younger children to the classroom on their first day of school. They help them get settled in and meet the teacher. At the end of the day they usually greet their child at the door to share in the big event. By the end of the first week most of the students have been weaned away from their parents (and parents from child) and have settled in to their regular transportation routines. Transitional information will need to be noted.
- Lunch routines may vary. It has been my experience that many young children (who do not receive free or reduced lunch) often bring their lunch from home on the first day. This seems to create more familiarity for the children. Their lunches are often packed with familiar well-liked foods, love notes, and special treats. They do not need to navigate themselves around the cafeteria and the lunch line, or deal with money. Too many new procedures or experiences can be overwhelming for some children. By the end of the week, children are usually confident enough with their own independence and learning to begin proudly venturing out to the adventures of the hot lunch line.
- Parent phone numbers may be different. On the first day of school many parents of younger children remain at the ready in case their child needs them. Some parents don't go to work at all that day and may be found at home if needed. Some parents may be out doing errands. Find out where the parents can be located on that specific day, just in case. There may be information you readily need that the child cannot communicate, such as how the child is getting home and what the child is doing for lunch.

It is important that during this transitional time we remain aware of all temporary information regarding each child. On the first day of school form, we will want to ask

- the child's name
- the parents' names (printed)
- where the parent can be reached
- home phone number

- emergency phone number for that first day, and the first week of school (this is also a good item to include on field trip forms)
- cell phone number
- pager number
- work number
- how the child is getting home, where he is meeting his ride, what the bus or daycare name and number are
- where the child's lunch is, where the child's lunch money is
- whether the child hase any allergies, medical needs, medicine, fears, nicknames, siblings in the building.

Although we may find this information in the child's permanent records, it is important to have at the ready on the first day. Some of the students may have school records still located at other school sites that will not be available the first week of school. Also, it takes a while for the school secretaries to complete and coordinate all of the student registration before the teacher receives it. This can be a very time-consuming process.

Parent Information Form

This form goes home with the child for the parent to fill out and return. Unlike the first day of school form, this form supplies you with the necessary permanent information on the parents and each child. On this form we want to include space for the following:

- child's name
- child's nickname
- parents' names (printed)
- home and work numbers
- cell phone and pager numbers
- emergency phone numbers
- child's age and birth date
- home mailing address
- parents' goals for their child during the school year
- anything else the parents think we should know: allergies, asthma, medications, divorce, custody issues, shyness, prior schooling or health problems, strengths, weaknesses, likes, dislikes, etc.
- volunteer information: who would like to volunteer in the classroom, what they would like to do, when they are available, whether they can do field trips.

Parent Letter

This is a welcome letter from you to the families. It establishes your tone for the school year and provides needed class and school information. I have found that the more thorough I am in my classroom introduction letter, the fewer inquiries I get and the less I need repeat myself later.

Being thorough in my letters also demonstrates that I respect the parents' desire to be aware and informed. I want my parents involved. I want them to understand what is going on in the classroom, and why. Younger children often do not communicate well about things that transpire at school. Informative letters are caring. Often, if the letter is long, I tell parents to read it at their leisure. My introduction welcome letters have contained the following:

- classroom schedules regarding school hours, lunch times, and days and times of special activities such as PE, art, library
- yearly themes, topics of study, and an overview of our quarterly inquiries and curriculum
- information regarding volunteering in the classroom
- information regarding visiting in the classroom/school
- snack time and snack procedures
- nap times and nap procedures
- information regarding a change of clothing in case of accidents
- information on keeping a paint shirt in school
- student drop-off and dismissal procedures
- PTO information
- upcoming school and class events
- cafeteria procedures and information regarding menus, lunch accounts, and eating with your child at school
- how the parents can contact me (parent/teacher journals)
- procedures for conferences
- homework procedures
- discipline policies
- grading and evaluation policies
- classroom routines
- class kudos and thank-you messages
- class wish list of needs and supplies
- fund-raisers
- volunteer sign-up times
- classroom supply list
- parent goals and expectations for students

- how to help the child at home
- things the child should know at his or her grade level
- a description of our reading/language arts program.

Student Information Form and Class Roster

We will want to create a student information form for the first day of school. This sheet is for our immediate reference and will be used frequently. I usually keep this sheet on a clipboard near my desk. In order to create our student information form, we must first create a class roster.

To make a class roster, you will need:

- a copy of your class list
- class roster template (Appendix C: Form 4f)

1. Using a copy of Form 4f, write each student's name in the first column.
2. That's it—you're done. Make several copies of this Class Roster. It can be used frequently throughout the year for varying purposes.

Note: I find it easier to list the children alphabetically by their first names. I often do not remember their last names during the first few days of school. This list provides a quick reference.

Now, using our class roster, let's create our student information sheet. Form 4e is an example of a student information form I have created and used in my classroom. If Form 4e suits your needs, then simply copy it. If it is not appropriate for your needs, then you will need to create your own headings. To do this you will need a copy of your class roster.

Across the top of your roster sheet, fill in the headings for the information you desire. These could include

- lunch account numbers
- student numbers
- bus numbers
- transportation modes
- dismissal routines
- lunch routines
- ages in years and months
- birth dates
- parents' names
- home phone numbers
- work numbers
- emergency numbers
- home mailing addresses
- special needs
- special services
- baseline test scores

When your headings are in place you are done. Make several copies of this template. It is helpful to keep one copy at home and one copy at school.

Class Supply List

Most schools have their teachers prepare a class supply list to go home with the families either at registration or on the first day of school. Some supply items I requested are

- pencils
- erasers
- markers (wide and narrow)
- dry-erase markers (set for each student)
- colored pencils
- crayons
- three-ring notebooks
- file folders
- white copy paper
- zippered plastic bags (gallon)
- spiral notebooks
- notebook paper
- scissors
- wet glue
- glue stick
- dry-erase board erasers
- camera film
- blank audio-tapes
- antibacterial soap
- tissues
- poster board
- paper towels
- Band-Aids
- snacks
- paper cups
- paper plates
- supply box
- backpack
- paint shirt
- stickie notes
- play dough

Record-Keeping and Management Materials
Often Used Forms and Checklists

You will want to create and duplicate various forms and checklists that will be frequently used in the classroom. Because these forms are used routinely, they are required in bulk. Unless you have unlimited access to a copier, you may want to take some of these forms to a printer and receive a bulk price. Some of the forms that I frequently use (all of which can be found in Appendix C) are

- Science Observation Form
- literature group contract
- Writing Workshop Status Checklist

- Mr. Bear Form
- lesson plan
- Literature Group Checklist
- daily/weekly performance class roster forms
- Class Job List

Lunch Number Clothespins

I write each child's name and his or her lunch account number onto a spring clothespin. The clothespins are stored in a basket or lunch box and retrieved by the child at lunch time. Children clip their number onto their clothes and do not hold up the lunch line or other students if they forget their number. This will help your students become more responsible, confident, and self-sufficient. It will also save you the time of last-minute searching when a child forgets her number.

> TEACHER'S NOTE: The clothespins also work well for identifying car riders, daycare students, and bus numbers. These same clothespins can also be used in graphing activities, such as How many more children take a bus than walk?

Vote for Lunch Area

Each day when my students enter the classroom, they sign in and then vote for lunch. To vote for lunch, students retrieve their magnets from the metal lunch box that is kept at the entrance to the classroom. On the wall in front of them are two cookie sheets. One cookie sheet is labeled "I brought my lunch to school." The other cookie sheet is labeled "I get my lunch at school." The children place their magnets on the appropriate cookie sheet. When attendance is taken, the helper of the day counts the number of children who are getting their lunch at school and records the number on our attendance sheet.

This lends itself to real-life word problem activities: Twelve students brought their lunch to school. Eleven children are getting their lunch at school. How many students are in class today? How do we know? How many more children brought their lunch than are buying?

To make a Vote for Lunch area we need:

- two cookie sheets
- adhesive-backed magnets, business card size (found at most office supply and copy centers)
- 2" x 3.5" white business cards (these can be purchased or cut from tagboard)

Directions:

1. Label one cookie sheet "I get my lunch at school."
2. Label the second cookie sheet "I brought my lunch to school."
3. On the first day of school, supply a business card magnet to each student. Have each child decorate his magnet with his name and a design.
4. Store in metal lunch box when completed.

Journals

I make my own journals for the primary grades of K–2. This allows me to adapt the paper to the activity and the child's developmental level. I have made journals using plain newsprint, storybook newsprint, white copy paper, and/or graph paper. I have found that journal covers made from tagboard or card stock, as compared to construction paper, hold up nicely throughout their use.

I usually add about fifty sheets of paper per journal and staple the tagboard covers in three places along the side. One of the best investments I have ever made for my classroom was a heavy-duty stapler for stapling materials of varying thickness. The stapler is great for making journals and class books.

Some of the journals I have used in my classroom are

- morning journals
- literature journals
- science logs
- math journals

- dialogue journals
- writing workshop logs
- compliment journals

Weekly Work Folders

I use three-prong paper folders as portfolios, logs, journals, and reports or to hold weekly work samples of the same nature. For example, each week my students complete a science observation. Each week my students also illustrate a poem. When a student completes her science observation or completes her poem, she immediately places it in her science or poetry folder. This allows me to see whose work is completed and the quality of the work, and allows me to observe work samples and growth over a period of time. The student gains the life skills of organization and responsibility.

Sign-In Book

Each child signs in when he enters our classroom in the morning. The sign-in book could be a journal or a spiral notebook. The date is written across the top of the page and attached to a clipboard. After the child signs in, he proceeds to vote for lunch.

Signing in allows me to see growth in students' writing over time, but it also allows me to see who remembers, who is responsible, and who is organized and follows classroom procedures.

Helper Calendar

I use a yearly calendar that is coordinated to our theme for recording the helper of the day each day. After I record the students in alphabetical order by their first names on the calendar, it is posted near our Class Job List and message board. The children are then able to see when their special day is coming. The helper of the day is the line leader, completes the morning calendar, and takes home Mr. Bear.

Because children enter and exit my class throughout the year, I complete the calendar one month at a time.

Figure 4–1. Sign-in table

Laminated Folders

I decorate and laminate different colored file folders that I use frequently throughout the year. This is a great organizational tool and record keeper. The files I create are titled

- Things to File
- Things to Copy
- Things to Disperse
- Master Copies
- Things I'm Working On
- Book Orders
- Papers to Grade

- Substitute Information/Guide
- Make-Up Work
- Clip Art (for yearly theme)
- Field Trip Forms
- Interim Reports
- Report Cards.

I also create folders to hold materials for each day's daily classroom activities. These folders are labeled with the days of the week.

Student Records and Files

Student Records (for Teacher)

I create a file folder for each student in my class. In this folder go all pertinent student materials throughout the year. This can include tardy slips, parent notes, signed papers, discipline forms, and so on. This is for my records and documentation only. They are kept with my teacher files and other assessments.

Student Work Samples

Each student has a file folder of class work samples that I keep throughout the year. I always make sure that I save materials from the beginning, middle, and end of the school year, as well as quarterly samples. This portfolio is for my records and assessment documentation and is kept with my teacher files.

Record-Keeping Notebook

I maintain a three-inch three-ring notebook for record keeping. The notebook is divided into sections. I utilize one section per student. In this notebook I keep all standardized test results, assessment results, screenings, and documents that pertain to each child throughout the year. These items usually end up as documentation in the student's cumulative folder at the end of the year. These items could include

- readiness tests
- baseline and theme tests
- school and district assessments
- computerized reading tests
- content chapter tests
- cumulative exams
- Internet use permission forms
- field trip blanket permission forms
- permission to be photographed forms
- home language survey forms
- drug addendum forms.

I also use the notebook to maintain my anecdotal records. I record my student observations onto shipping labels that I keep attached to a clipboard throughout the day (see Figure 4–2). I use one label per student. After I date the observation, I peel off the label and attach it to the student's section in the record-keeping notebook.

Writing Workshop Portfolio/Notebook

My younger children (K–2) organize and maintain their writing drafts, samples, and finished products in several different ways. Depending upon the intent of the lesson, the type of finished product, the duration of the project, and the space available, we save and store our work differently. Sometimes we utilize

- file folders
- pocket folders
- gallon zippered bags
- stapled poster board portfolios
- stapled construction paper pouches
- plastic baskets

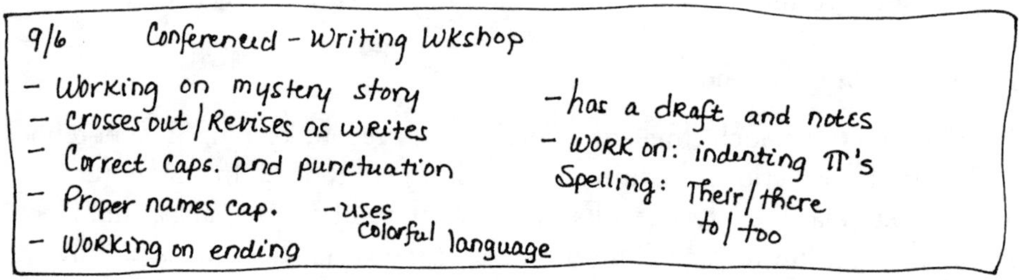
9/6 Conferenced - Writing Wkshop
- Working on mystery story
- crosses out / Revises as writes
- Correct caps. and punctuation
- Proper names cap.
- Working on ending
- uses colorful language
- has a draft and notes
- Work on: indenting ¶'s
Spelling: Their/there
to/too

Figure 4–2. Anecdotal record

- soda flats
- hanging big book bags
- filing cabinet drawers
- notebooks
- composition books
- classroom display.

Often children in kindergarten and first grade do very little editing and revising in their writing. In stories, their written work tends to reflect more energy in the illustrations and publishing than the choice of words for the text. They love to illustrate their stories not only with crayons and markers also with 3D sculptures and elaborate book concepts. Their work needs to be kept safe until they are finished. Because of size and student desire, writing products from the younger children usually go home regularly. However, it's important to not let the publishing and illustrating of a book override the intent of writing workshop or writing daily. Depending on your intent, a good rule to follow is that writers only illustrate and publish when their story is completed.

In third through sixth grades the students maintain their writing in a three-inch three-ring notebook. This becomes their writing workshop notebook. Maintaining the notebook is part of the students' grade and responsibility. The rules in writing workshop maintain that students write daily, date all work, erase nothing, and throw nothing away. This notebook therefore serves as an ongoing assessment of each student's writing development throughout the year.

Students' finished pieces can be published, dated, and maintained in the class library, school library, or student portfolio. Writing workshop notebooks, storage boxes, or file folders may need to be readied for the children before school starts.

Reading Journals/Logs

Students in grades 3 through 6 maintain a reading log, or journal. This journal is usually a spiral notebook that is used to record responses to literature read throughout the year. This log serves as an ongoing assessment of the student's behaviors with print. Reading journals may need to be purchased and/or labeled.

Yearly Assessments

Required Assessments

I set up and maintain a three-inch three-ring notebook for required yearly assessments. At the beginning of the year I identify all of the required assessments from each content area that need to be administered for accountability and placed in the child's cumulative folder at the end of the school year. These usually include

- kindergarten readiness tests
- vision and hearing screenings
- reading and math baselines
- required content unit tests and/or theme tests
- beginning and ending writing samples.

I then make a copy of each test, test administration directions, and the date the test is to be administered. These tests are then placed either chronologically or by content into my assessment notebook. When the test is completed, it then goes into the student's section of my record-keeping notebook.

Other Assessments

I keep all nonrequired assessments and informal assessments organized by subject matter in a file drawer. This includes remaining theme and unit tests, inventory tests, miscue analysis materials, running record forms, informal reading inventories, Dolch words, concepts of print materials, guided reading materials, and open-ended critical thinking literature probes, which are used for lessons, modeling, and evaluation.

Miscellaneous Managerial Items

MATERIALS TO MAKE AND CREATE
- student seating arrangement
- desk tags
- nametags
- hall passes: library, office, clinic
- school and classroom procedures: written procedures for daily class and school routines such as morning procedures, carpet procedures, dismissal procedures, cafeteria procedures, playground procedures, writing workshop procedures, etc.

TEACHER SUPPLIES TO GATHER FOR CLASSROOM
- pencils with erasers
- markers
- black ink pens
- batteries
- soap
- paper towels

- felt-tip pens
- overhead transparency markers
- dry-erase markers
- white board erasers
- chalk
- chalk erasers
- electric pencil sharpener
- ruler
- yardstick
- measuring tape
- CD or cassette player
- staplers
- staples
- transparent tape
- masking tape
- rubber bands
- rubber gloves
- Band-Aids
- clinic passes
- paper clips
- pushpins
- hole punch
- three-hole punch
- camera
- antibacterial soap
- varied sizes of zippered plastic bags
- stickie notes
- spring clothespins
- yearly calendar
- first day snacks
- attendance slips
- map of school
- school phone extension numbers
- construction paper
- writing paper
- transparencies
- transparencies for the copy machine
- envelopes
- note cards
- memo pads
- paper cutter
- scissors
- plastic grocery sacks
- 9"x12" clasp envelopes
- file folders
- clipboards

Finishing Touches

- Appendix C: Form 4c
- Appendix C: Form 4d

5
Teaching Throughout the Year

In this final chapter we will focus upon considerations, experiences, and obligations that we will encounter throughout the school year. We will look at

- curriculum issues throughout the year:
    why the first month's curriculum and scheduling need to be different
    observing and documenting growth over time
    accommodating new students
- communicating with parents:
    open house
    newsletters
    conferences
    daily/weekly communication
- preparing for a substitute
- what it means to be a professional:
    what a professional teacher looks like?
    student advocacy and teacher responsibilities
- helpful hints (some time-tested suggestions from the *front line*).

Let's begin this chapter by returning once more to our curriculum.

Curriculum Issues and Concerns

In this section we will look at our completed curriculum and examine the changes and adaptations we need to make during those first days and weeks of school. We will need to determine what we are going to teach the first day of school, how we are going to introduce our programs, how we are going to build community, how we are going to establish classroom procedures and expectations, and how the beginning of the year brings changes in our teaching, scheduling, and activities.

Getting Through the First Month of School

Changes in Teaching Schedule and Activities
It's important to remember that the first weeks of school are often not reflective of the remainder of the school year. There are certain activities that take place (or don't take place) during this first month of school that will affect your scheduling and teaching. For example:

- Some special activities, clubs, sports, or extra labs, such as computer, media, chorus, student government, and band, may not be prepared to begin during the first week of school.
- Student services such as Title I, occupational therapy, speech, special education resources, and guidance will most likely have to review and assess former students as well as screen and assess new students. Some services may not start until well into the second or third week of school.
- Some schools have required testing at the beginning of the school year. Some of these assessments may need to be given by the teacher, while other assessments will need to be administered by other parties. Some of these could include
   baseline content tests
   readiness tests
   modality tests
   vision tests
   hearing tests
   computerized reading tests
   informal reading inventories (includes miscue analysis,
      interest inventories, and running records)
   ability tests
   standardized achievement tests.
- Some schools have special beginning-of-the-year activities, such as
   fund-raiser assemblies
   school pep rallies
   school pictures
   fire, bus, and bike safety assemblies and presentations
   red ribbon week (antidrug campaign).

All of these activities will determine your scheduling for the day; you may have to work around conflicting lunch schedules and special activity schedules. *Flexibility, patience,* and *a sense of humor* during the first month of school are often the key to remaining calm and sane. Expect the unexpected to pop up and be ready to happily adapt for it at any given time.

Remember, during these first few weeks of school, we as teachers will also have to be flexible and adapt within our own established classroom structures:

- Our class roster may change several times due to late registrations, transfers, or mobility of students.
- We should expect our scheduling to change frequently as we determine timing and the personalities and needs of the students.
- We may rethink and alter our entire curriculum, procedures, and/or content studies once we meet our students.
- We may wish to rearrange our room to make it more functional.
- We may have our own assessments, baselines, inventories, observations, inquiries, work samples, and/or evaluations that may cause changes in our thinking, scheduling, and curriculum structures.

Change during this time period is not a negative. In fact, it is a sign of growth and should be viewed as continuous learning and reflection.

Sample Beginning-of-the-Year Schedule
During the first month of school I primarily focus upon getting to know the children, modeling and establishing classroom procedures, and completing all needed beginning-of-the-year assessments. For the younger grades that entails creating their school folders and providing all baseline testing and home documentations.

Testing in the younger grades usually includes a school readiness test for kindergarteners, a baseline reading test from the school reading series, a baseline math test from the school math series, a beginning-of-the-year writing sample, and probably some type of reading inventory such as a guided reading level, a running record, miscue analysis, or a computerized program.

In the intermediate grades there are normally baseline tests for most subject areas, a computerized test, and a beginning-of-the-year writing sample.

I have found that the best way to prepare for the first few weeks of school is to maintain my scheduling time frames for routine and structure and weave in the testing and daily changes as needed. I am not even concerned about initiating the actual content of our yearly theme yet. This will come in time. During the first few weeks of school, rather than actual lesson plans, I maintain long lists of what needs to be accomplished throughout the days and week.

My lesson plans during this time would look something like this:

8:15–8:30	Organize for day
8:30–8:45	Morning procedures, begin modeling morning journal writing and sharing procedures
8:45–Lunch	Class meeting/welcome
	Shared reading
	Poem
	Introduce morning calendar
	Reading workshop
	Writing workshop
	Work on To Do list
11:13–11:40	Lunch
11:40–12:00	Bathrooms, drinks, short recess
12:00–12:25	Teacher read-aloud
12:25–1: 25	Work on To Do list
1:25–2:05	Special activity/planning
2:05–2:30	Work on To Do list
2:30–2:55	Classroom jobs
	Organize and clean for home
	Share on carpet/closing of day
2:55–3:15	Dismissal

To Do List

1. Mr. Bear
2. helper of the day
3. writing sample
4. classroom exploration
5. classroom and school procedures
6. safety issues: fire drills
7. class jobs
8. baseline testing: math
9. baseline testing: reading
10. model writing workshop procedures
11. model reading workshop procedures
12. cooperative learning activities/ math
13. science observations
14. using classroom materials
15. class library checkout
16. lunch numbers
17. transportation clarity
18. voting for lunch
19. interest inventories

Every day and evening I go through my To Do list and add items that crop up and delete items that have been completed. Little by little things will get done as needed. In the meantime, the students are being introduced to participating in the class staples and routines of organizing and being responsible for supplies, shared reading time, reading workshop, writing workshop, morning journals, morning procedures, morning calendar, teacher read-aloud, Mr. Bear, envelope books, science observations, and class jobs. If by some chance the school nurse pops in to weigh and measure the children or take them for a vision test, then I have options (depending upon the time and need) to go to my To Do list or work on one of our routines that needs reinforcement and practice, such as writing workshop, discussing books, and so on. The children also get an opportunity to visit and experience classroom areas throughout the day, allowing some time for free exploration.

By the end of the second or third week, all beginning-of-the-year school business should be completed for the most part. Our schedule becomes more stable and routine, and content knowledge from our curriculum becomes slowly introduced into our established routines.

Classroom Community, Procedures, and Expectations
During this expected time of flexibility we are busy in our classrooms working on our first two priorities: building our community and establishing classroom procedures and expectations. This is our time to

1. Get to know the students while we reflect upon our setting, curriculum, and predetermined procedures. Observe the class as a whole to determine your classroom dynamics, interest, abilities, and socialization. Constantly kidwatch to see how each child interacts, participates, and displays interest; whether he is organized, responsible, and trustworthy; and whether he remembers and follows procedures, demonstrates motivation, and actively listens.

   Pay attention to their demonstrated abilities as well as the types of behaviors displayed during activities. For example, is the student uncomfortable when it comes to reading? Does she panic during tests? Need help holding scissors? Avoids participating in calendar? Like to write? Wander the room? Push and butt in line? Recall directions? Complete work quickly and with little effort? Demonstrate personal best? Work independently?

2. Allow the students time to feel comfortable and confident with their new setting, materials, procedures, classmates, teacher, and expectations.

3. Model, reinforce, and support all class procedures, routines, rules, and expectations. Include and practice the regular routines daily. Go slowly and

provide continuous feedback throughout the tasks and at the time of their completion. Give examples of what outstanding, good, satisfactory, and average work for each task looks like. Have the children help determine if all criteria were met for each activity. Work together to see who needs help, build upon individual strengths, create risk taking, and help each child successfully complete each activity before the student is required to complete the activity individually and/or for a grade or assessment.

Begin by doing every activity as a whole class. When the class understands the concept, move to small-group work, buddy work, and then independent work. These are all practices and attempts. Therefore, the work during this time period should not be graded. This is a time for feedback, support, and creating risk taking and trust. In my classroom there are no mistakes; errors are referred to as *attempts, learning, practicing,* and *applying effort.* All student work during this stage is praised for trying and perseverance. We then look at how we can make the students' work stronger or better.

4. Build caring, trust, and risk taking among the students. Establish caring as your number one rule and stick to it. Be fair, be consistent, problem solve instead of yell, offer alternative choices, reinforce and build upon the positive, teach children alternative ways to express their anger, hold class meetings, discuss how various behaviors make us feel, discuss how our feelings affect our learning, talk to each child daily, begin with a lot of successful materials, utilize various cooperative groupings, utilize whole-class lessons and small-group work, allow the children time to socialize and get to know each other, model appropriate ways to converse and be a good audience, accept all students equally, have fun, and let each child know that you care about him or her personally and academically. Students must believe that you love them and are on their side. They must trust you with their fears, insecurities, vulnerabilities, and safety. Love your students, and love them quickly.

5. Allow the students ownership over some of the classroom environment, structure, scheduling, rules, content, materials, consequences, and procedures. Allow and invite the students to generate their thoughts on these matters. I have three major rules in my classroom:
    a. The children will be caring.
    b. The children will try their personal best.
    c. The children will use integrity and be responsible for their learning.
    Other than that, I discuss most issues that require behavioral procedures with the class. We have decided upon discipline procedures for uncompleted work, verbal rudeness, lack of responsibility, and physically hurting

another student. We have created acceptable playground behaviors, rules for the bathroom and sink areas, and rules for carpet sharing time and have even voted upon our daily agenda.

6. Allow the students options and choice whenever appropriate and possible.

Remember, the time spent now building our class community and modeling procedures is invaluable to the way that the rest of the school year progresses. Don't worry about suspending some of the specific curriculum content during this time period. Until the students feel safe, secure, and valued, learning will not take place. Once we have a child's trust and respect, we can help her learn anything.

Observing and Documenting Growth Over Time

Most of the documentation we need for observing growth and learning over time is already built into our classroom structure. We have authentic samples of the students' writing and language skills from the beginning of the year until the end of the year in each student's writing workshop notebook, reading response log, and/or morning journals. As discussed in Chapter 4, our reading logs, checklists, and records of students' readings provide us with information regarding comprehension, approximate independent and instructional reading levels, reading behaviors and motivation, choice of genres, use of predominant reading strategies, sense of story structure, concept of print, vocabulary development, spelling, handwriting, sequencing, effort, responsibility, risk taking, and applied skills (checklists of expected skills, goals, and class recording sheets are located in Appendix C).

It is also possible to compare a student's growth throughout the year by

- documenting all standards and benchmarks that were successfully demonstrated
- counting the number of sight words from the beginning of the year until the end of the year
- comparing the word count, conventional spellings, and story development from writing workshop at the beginning of the year to the end of the year.

Additional work samples, observations, and periodic informal and formal testing provide balance and a variety of information from different domains that complete our picture of the student over time.

Accommodating New Students

Accommodating new students throughout the year is usually not a problem if we remember to make and keep at the ready extra copies of parent letters, folders, forms, journals, and curriculum materials from the beginning of the school year.

The easiest way to accomplish this is to simply add space for five unknown students to our class list at the beginning of the school year. While creating materials needed for our actual student count (lunch magnets, nametags, journals, crayons, class curriculum info, student information forms, etc.), we can make five additional packages and keep them on file in the classroom. If a new student enters during the year, we simply pull a premade class package from our filing cabinet. This saves us from searching for and re-creating various needed materials and information. It is always a good idea to seat the new student next to a responsible class member who can function as his helper (and yours) throughout the first couple of days.

We will also need to check with the school secretary in charge of records to see if the student's cumulative school file has been received from the student's prior school or school district. There may be testing measures required by our district or school that we must administer to the new student. It is also a good idea to see where the student left off in his prior learning and previous report cards, and to see if there were any prior or ongoing special education testing and/or services, IEPs, or 504 documents.

Communication with Parents

Open House

Open House generally occurs within the first two or three weeks of school. The purpose of Open House is for the parents to get to meet you, view the classroom, and hear information from you regarding the class or the classroom. It is not a time to conference or discuss individual student needs and observations with parents. Some items to discuss at Open House could include

- daily class schedule
- special activity and lunch schedule
- classroom rules
- classroom procedures
- classroom reading program

- evaluation and assessment of grades
- student responsibilities
- ways parents can help their child at home
- what your curricular focuses will be throughout the year
- classroom needs
- volunteers, room mothers
- the necessity of checking the child's backpack daily
- snacks, supplies, quiet time, dismissal.

Newsletters and Daily/Weekly Communications

I find that the more proactive and open we are with our parents, the easier our job will become throughout the year. I spend a great deal of time at the beginning of the year explaining my program, procedures, evaluation, and philosophy and providing updates from the classroom. Parents of younger children particularly appreciate this because frequently the children cannot verbalize the information accurately, or they misunderstand and are confused. It also helps build a working rapport and relationship between the school and the home. The parents feel included in and apprised of all situations. I give each parent a spiral-bound notebook to be used as a parent-teacher journal for communication throughout the year. The notebook contains a cover label stating my name, school address, grade, school email address, and school phone number. This journal is kept at home and brought to school by the child when the parent wishes to communicate with me. I usually respond after school and the journal goes back home with the child the next day. Usually I am asked about classroom needs, updates on children's behavior and academics, confusion, or setting up a conference—and on a good day, there may just be a letter of thanks and support. In addition, newsletters contain class info and announcements, class news, spotlights on children or volunteers, and samples of students' work (see some samples in Appendix C).

Conferences

There are three types of conferences that I employ:
    parent-teacher
    parent-student-teacher
    student-led.

Each conference serves a different purpose and accomplishes different needs. I use parent-teacher conferences when I wish to speak openly and candidly about a child's progress without the child within earshot. This is usually employed on an as-needed basis if I have concerns regarding performance, wish to discuss a child study meeting, or if the parent has information of a personal nature that the child should not hear.

I utilize parent-student-teacher conferences when discussing general classroom performance, work samples, classroom behaviors, attitudes, growth, things to work on, and at times when we need to sit down and draw up a contract, problem solve a behavior, or build a student's confidence. Three-way conferences can be scheduled as needed, or they can be utilized as part of schoolwide conference evenings. I find that three-way conferences also work very well when there are discrepancies regarding what is happening at school and what is being reported at home.

Student-led conferences allow the student time to demonstrate and show off what she has learned and/or is working on in the classroom. Student-led conferences can be held simultaneously (about five at a time) in a workshop/centerlike setting. Create areas throughout the room where children sit with their parents and share their work and/or demonstrate a new skill or new knowledge. Areas could include

- morning calendar
- writing workshop portfolio
- morning journals
- reading a book
- responding to a book
- a science observation
- math centers.

Often, I schedule student-led conferences on a Saturday and make the event a class family share day with various displayed work samples and, of course, music, food, and snacks. The parents are usually not rushed for time and it allows the families and students an opportunity to visit and share. I try to schedule a family day every quarter. If this becomes impossible, then we'll have a student-led conference every semester.

Depending upon your school, it may not be necessary to get prior approval from the school principal. However, I have always found it best to run the idea past the principal and secure verbal approval. I think that principals should be aware of any activities occurring in your classroom outside of school hours. There may be issues regarding school insurance, security, and/or unforeseen consequences. It's best to ask.

Substitute Preparations

Planning for a substitute includes more than just leaving clear and concise plans, directions, and materials. More goes into the management of our classrooms than just time schedules and content. Instead of re-creating the wheel every time we are out of the building, it is best to create a substitute information folder as close to the beginning of the school year as possible. This folder should contain

- updated class list
- established classroom rules (couch and pillows, bathroom rules)
- established classroom procedures (jobs, line leader, helper of the day, drinks, snacks)
- procedures for calendar, Mr. Bear, writing workshop, reading workshop
- dismissal procedures
- emergency procedures and maps
- clinic passes
- referral passes
- names of children who know certain procedures who can help the substitute (use of certain materials, areas in the classroom, teacher supplies, calendar, and the way things usually work)
- names of children who are trustworthy
- names of children who are afraid of the dark, fire drills, new people, etc.
- medical issues
- behavior concerns (who to watch, how they are usually disciplined, what works, who to get for help)
- mode of transportation home for each student
- school procedures for special activities, lunch, playground, etc.
- ways to work with certain children
- names of people at school who can help answer a question
- names of teachers on your grade level and/or team
- map of school
- phone extension numbers
- outside or dismissal duties before and after school
- names of children who attend special classes or activities during school hours
- attendance and lunch forms
- student nametags
- seating chart
- procedures for difficult students: where/who to send or call
- a comment sheet for substitute notes at the end of the day.

Keep the substitute folder in plain view near your desk at all times, and update the information on curriculum, schedules, and students throughout the year. Now, when you are out of the building you only need make curriculum plans for that certain day. The rest of your needed classroom information is in place in the substitute folder.

Professionalism

What a Professional Teacher Looks Like?

A professional teacher is a teacher who is organized, knows her curriculum, knows her students, and is well prepared. We dress respectfully and behave respectfully. Papers and documents are returned to other staff members on time. Courtesy is applied in both our voice and our actions. We plan ahead, are on time, and follow all school procedures. We do not gossip or randomly complain. Instead we take the source of our concern and our solutions to the person or people who can help rectify the situation. We stay current and grow in our field of education by reading professional materials, attending workshops, taking classes, sharing ideas, joining professional organizations, and building a rapport with the parents and community.

Student Advocacy and Teacher Responsibilities

As a professional we also maintain the responsibility of being an advocate for our students. This means that we are on their side and are working for their best interests at all times. This includes

- knowing the federal and state laws regarding student services and proactively securing them as needed
- knowing your students' strengths and zones of proximal development
- modifying curriculum and materials
- knowing and evaluating what learning looks like in an authentic context
- making the students successful on standardized materials
- representing and advocating for the students in all formal and informal discussions pertaining to their academic and behavioral needs and performance
- possibly going up against the school system, court system, and colleagues on behalf of your students
- gaining the trust of the students and parents
- treating and fighting for the students as a mother would her own child
- understanding reading, writing, literacy, and language processes and acquisition.

Figure 5–1. Aram Hebert (age 6)

Helpful Hints

The following is a list of some classroom hints that have proved valuable throughout the years:

- Never send more than two to four children into the bathroom at one time while being monitored.
- Never send more than one child into the bathroom at a time when not being monitored.
- Always count your students, even when you think it unnecessary.

- Check for sleeping children or children in bathroom before leaving the classroom.
- Never leave the children unattended.
- Always tell the special activity teacher how many children you are leaving in his care.
- Keep regularly used forms, logos, letterheads, and certificates on your hard drive and a floppy.
- If you do not have a computer and plan to buy one, it is helpful to get a home computer that is compatible with the computers and software used at school.
- Copy anything and everything before submitting it to any school secretary, administrator, parent, or district employee.
- Keep a conference log. Include phone conferences and impromptu meetings.
- Make the secretaries and custodians your best friends.
- Don't gossip, especially in the teachers lounge.
- Choose a fire drill line leader and end-of-line person at the beginning of the school year. Show the line leader where to start walking and wait for you while you grab your plan book and keys. Have the end-of-the-line person shut the lights off and close the door.
- Establish jobs. Include line leader, escort, door holder, and end-of-line person.
- Establish procedures for who gets the couch and pillows, and when it's allowed.
- Don't buy everything you like.
- Be proactive.
- Try not to take parent remarks or student behavior, performance, and attitude personally.
- A good filing system is essential.
- Don't try to do everything at once. Implement new routines and methods only as you feel comfortable.
- Be flexible.
- Maintain balance: you must still have a home life, hobbies, and friends.
- Know that every day is a rough draft.
- Learn to laugh at yourself.

Appendix A: Resources

Professional Resources

The following is my short list of required professional readings and/or authors. These books are tried and true. They have inspired, supported, challenged, and influenced my knowledge, thought processes, questions, inquiries, and risk taking.

Reading: Theory, Research, and Practice

Allington, R. L., and S. A. Walmsley. 1995. *No Quick Fix.* Newark, DE: International Reading Association.

Cambourne, B. 1988. *The Whole Story: Natural Learning and the Acquisition of Literacy in the Classroom.* New York: Scholastic.

Daniels, H. 1994. *Literature Circles: Voice and Choice in the Student-Centered Classroom.* York, ME: Stenhouse.

Fountas, I. C., and G. S. Pinnell. 1996. *Guided Reading: Good First Teaching for All Children.* Portsmouth, NH: Heinemann.

———. 1999. *Matching Books to Readers.* Portsmouth, NH: Heinemann.

Goodman, K. 1996. *On Reading: A Common-Sense Look at the Nature of Language and the Science of Reading.* Portsmouth, NH: Heinemann.

Goodman, Y., D. Watson, and C. Burke. 1987. *Reading Miscue Inventory: Alternative Procedures.* New York: Richard C. Owens.

Goodman, Y. and G. Owocki. 2002. *Kidwatching: Documenting Children's Literacy Developments.* Portsmouth, N.H.: Heinemann.

Johnson, T. D., and D. R. Louis. 1987. *Literacy Through Literature.* Portsmouth, NH: Heinemann.

Norton, D. E., and S. E. Norton. 1999. *Through the Eyes of a Child.* 5th ed. Columbus, OH: Merrill.

Peterson, R., and M. Eeds. 1990. *Grand Conversations*. New York: Scholastic.

Rosenblatt, L. 1938. *Literature as Exploration*. New York: Modern Language Association.

———. 1978. *The Reader, the Text, the Poem*. Carbondale, IL: Southern Illinois University Press.

Short, K. G., and K. M. Pierce. 1990. *Talking About Books: Creating Literate Communities*. Portsmouth, NH: Heinemann.

Short, K. G., J. Harste, and C. Burke. 1996. *Creating Classrooms for Authors and Inquirers*. 2nd ed. Portsmouth, NH: Heinemann.

Tunnell, M. O., and J. S. Jacobs. 2000. *Children's Literature, Briefly*. 2nd ed. Columbus, OH: Merrill/Prentice Hall.

Weaver, C. 2002. *Reading Process and Practice*. 3rd ed. Portsmouth, NH: Heinemann.

Writing: Theory, Research, and Practice

Atwell, N. 1990. *Coming to Know: Writing to Learn in the Intermediate Grades*. Portsmouth, NH: Heinemann.

———. 1998. *In the Middle: Reading and Learning with Adolescents*. 2nd ed. Portsmouth, NH: Heinemann.

Calkins, L. M. 1991. *Living Between the Lines*. Portsmouth, NH: Heinemann.

Chancer, J., and G. Rester-Zodrow. 1997. *Moon Journals: Writing, Art, and Inquiry Through Focused Nature Study*. Portsmouth, NH: Heinemann.

Dyson, A. 1989. *Multiple Worlds of Child Writers: Friends Learning to Write*. New York: Teacher's College Press.

Graves, D. 1983. *Writing: Teachers and Children at Work*. Portsmouth, NH: Heinemann.

———. 1994. *A Fresh Look at Writing*. Portsmouth, NH: Heinemann.

Skills, Strategies, Word Work, Phonics, Spelling

Bear, D. R., M. Invernizzi, F. Johnston, and S. Templeton. 1996. *Words Their Way*. Columbus, OH: Merrill.

Cunningham, P. 2000. *Phonics They Use: Words for Reading and Writing*. 3rd ed. New York: Addison-Wesley.

Cunningham, P., and D. Hall. 1994. *Making Words*. Torrance, CA: Good Apple.

———. 1997. *Making More Words*. Torrance, CA: Good Apple.

Goodman, K. 1993. *Phonics Phacts*. Portsmouth, NH: Heinemann.

Marriott, D. 1997. *What Are the Other Kids Doing . . . While You Teach Small Groups*. Cypress, CA: Creative Teaching.

Moustafa, M. 1997. *Beyond Traditional Phonics*. Portsmouth, NH: Heinemann.

Pinnell, G. S., and I. C. Fountas. 1998. *Word Matters*. Portsmouth, NH: Heinemann.

Wilde, S. 1997. *What's a Schwa Sound Anyway?* Portsmouth, NH: Heinemann.

Comprehensive, Balanced, Literacy Instruction

Avery, C. 1993. *And with a Light Touch: Learning About Reading, Writing, and Teaching with First Graders*. Portsmouth, NH: Heinemann.

Clay, M. 1991. *Becoming Literate*. Portsmouth, NH: Heinemann.

Cunningham, P. M., and R. L. Allington. 1999. *Classrooms That Work: They Can All Read and Write*. 2nd ed. New York: Longman.

Daniels, H., and M. Bizar. 1998. *Methods That Matter*. York, ME: Stenhouse.

Elkind, D. 1988. *The Hurried Child*. 2nd ed. New York: Addison-Wesley.

Fisher, B. 1995. *Thinking and Learning Together*. Portsmouth, NH: Heinemann.

———. 1996. *Inside the Classroom: Teaching Kindergarten and First Grade*. Portsmouth, NH: Heinemann.

Goodlad, J. I. 1984. *A Place Called School*. New York: McGraw-Hill.

Pappas, C. C., B. Z. Kiefer, and L. S. Levstik. 1990. *An Integrated Perspective in the Elementary School: Theory into Action*. White Plains, New York: Longman.

Rhodes, L. K., and N. L. Shanklin. 1993. *Windows into Literacy*. Portsmouth, NH: Heinemann.

Routman, R. 1988. *Transitions*. Portsmouth, NH: Heinemann.

———. 1994. *Invitations*. 2nd ed. Portsmouth, NH: Heinemann.

———. 2000. *Conversations*. Portsmouth, NH: Heinemann.

Taylor, D. 1993. *From a Child's Point of View*. Portsmouth, NH: Heinemann.

Vygotsky, L. S. 1978. *Mind in Society*. Cambridge, MA: Harvard University Press.

Learning Disabilities, Advocacy, and Mainstreaming

Coughlin, D. 2000. *The Mainstreaming Handbook*. Portsmouth, NH: Heinemann.

Rhodes, L. K., and C. Dudley-Marling. 1996. *Readers and Writers with a Difference: A Holistic Approach to Teaching Struggling Readers*. 2nd ed. Portsmouth, NH: Heinemann.

Taylor, D. 1991. *Learning Denied*. Portsmouth, NH: Heinemann.

Taylor, D., D. Coughlin, and J. Marasco. 1997. *Teaching and Advocacy*. York, ME: Stenhouse.

Political Action and Critical Pedagogy

Bloom, B. 1956. *Taxonomy of Educational Objectives, Handbook 1: Cognitive Domain*. New York: McKay.

Goodman, K. 1998. *In Defense of Good Teaching*. York, ME: Stenhouse.

Goodman, K., P. Shannon, Y. Freeman, and S. Murphy. 1988. *Report Card on Basal Readers*. Katonah, New York: Richard C. Owen.

Pinar, W., H. Giroux, and A. N. Penna. eds. 1981. *Curriculum and Instruction: Alternatives in Education*. Berkeley, CA: McCutchan.

Routman, R. 1996. *Literacy at the Crossroads*. Portsmouth, NH: Heinemann.

Smith, F. 1986. *Insult to Intelligence*. Portsmouth, NH: Heinemann.

Taylor, D. 1998. *Beginning to Read and the Spin Doctors of Science.* Urbana, IL: National Council of Teachers of English.

Additional Professional Books: Content Resources

Reading

Kelly, J. 1992. *On Location: Settings from Famous Children's Books—#1.* Englewood, CO: Teacher Ideas.

Math

Baratta-Lorton, M. 1995. *Mathematics Their Way.* New York: Addison-Wesley.

Burns, M. 1992. *Math and Literature.* White Plains, New York: Math Solutions.

Equals. 1989. *Get It Together.* Berkeley, CA: Lawrence Hall of Science.

Social Studies and Science

Barchers, S. I., and P. C. Marden. 1991. *Cooking Up U.S. History.* Englewood, CO: Teacher Ideas.

Butzow, C. M., and J. Butzow. 1989. *Science Through Children's Literature.* Englewood, CO: Teacher Ideas.

Caduto, M. J., and J. Bruchac. 1989. *Keepers of the Earth.* Golden, CO: Fulcrum.

———. 1991. *Keepers of the Animals.* Golden, CO: Fulcrum.

———. 1994. *Keepers of the Night.* Golden, CO: Fulcrum.

Chancer, J., and G. Rester-Zodrow. 1997. *Moon Journals: Writing, Art, and Inquiry Through Focused Nature Study.* Portsmouth, NH: Heinemann.

Gail, J., and L. A. Houlding. 1995. *Day of the Moon Shadow.* Englewood, CO: Teacher Ideas.

Catalogs

The following companies have additional resources that I have used for classroom and literacy materials: software, pocket charts, furniture, storybook characters and manipulatives, puppets, word study, word searches, hidden pictures, write and read paper storybooks, sight word paper storybooks, classroom ideas, poetry, integrated units, word families, critical thinking, materials for substitutes, and test-taking practice.

Carson-Dellosa Publishing
Greensboro, NC 27425

Classroom Direct
P.O. Box 830677
Birmingham, AL 35283-0677
1-800-248-9171
www.classroomdirect.com

Copycat Press, Inc.
P.O. Box 081546
Racine, WI 53408-1546
www.copycatpress.com

Frank Schaffer Publications
23740 Hawthorne Blvd.
Torrence, CA 90505

Good Apple (A Frank Schaffer Publication)
23740 Hawthorne Blvd.
Torrence, CA 90505

Interact: A Learning Experience
1914 Palomar Oaks Way, Suite 150
Carlsbad, CA 92008
www.interact-simulations.com

Lakeshore Learning Materials
2695 E. Dominguez St.
Carson, CA 90810
1-800-421-5354
www.lakeshorelearning.com

Mindware
121 5th Ave. NW
New Brighton, MN 55112
1-800-999-0398
www.MINDWAREonline.com

Scholastic Professional Books
555 Broadway
New York, NY 10012
1-800-SCHOLASTIC
www.scholastic.com

Teaching Resource Center
P.O. Box 82777
San Diego, CA 92138
www.trcabc.com

Professional Organizations and Journals

National Council of Teachers of English (NCTE)
1111 W. Kenyon Road
Urbana, IL 61801-1096
877-369-6283
www.ncte.org
Journals: Primary Voices K–6; Language Arts; English Journal

Whole Language Umbrella (WLU)
National Council of Teachers of English
1111 W. Kenyon Road
Urbana, IL 61801-1096
www.ncte.org/wlu
Journal: *Talking Points*

International Reading Association (IRA)
800 Barksdale Road
P.O. Box 8139
Newark, DE 19714-8139
Journals: Reading Research Quarterly (*www.reading.org*); *The Reading Teacher*

Additional Professional Journals
Rethinking Schools
Rethinking Schools Limited
1001 East Keefe Ave.
Milwaukee, WI 53012
1-800-669-4192
www.rethinkingschools.org

The New Advocate
Christopher-Gordon Publishers, Inc.
1502 Providence Highway, Suite 12
Norwood, MA 02062

Phi Delta Kappan
408 N. Union St.
P.O. Box 789
Bloomington, IN 47402

Classroom Book Clubs

Scholastic Book Club now incorporates *Trumpet Book Club* and *Carnival Book Club*.
With one phone call or email, you can obtain all three catalogs and services:
1-800-SCHOLASTIC (1-800-724-6527)
www.scholastic.com

Magazines for Children

Kids Discover
170 Fifth Ave.
New York, NY 10010

National Geographic World
National Geographic Society
Washington, D.C. 20036

Ranger Rick
National Wildlife Association
8925 Leesburg, Pike
Vienna, VA 22184
www.nwf.org/nwf

Sports Illustrated for Kids
Time, Inc.
Time & Life Building, Rockefeller Center
New York, NY 10020-1393
www.sikids.com

Time for Kids
Time, Inc.
Time & Life Building, Rockefeller Center
New York, NY 10020-1393
www.timeforkids.com

Zoobooks
Wildlife Education Ltd.
12233 Thatcher Court
Poway, CA 92064-6880
www.zoobooks.com

Frequently Used Web Sites

Amazon.com
www.amazon.com

The Children's Literature Web Guide
www.acs.ucalgary.cal-dkbrown/

Great Sites: annotated listings of websites for classrooms and children
www.ala.org/parentspage/greatsites/amazing.html

Heinemann Publications
www.heinemann.com

Library of Congress
www.loc.gov/

Stenhouse Publications
www.stenhouse.com

Yahooligans
www.yahooligans.com

Literature

Favorite Authors and Illustrators: Picture Books

Jim Arnosky	Leo Lionni
Graeme Base	Jonathan London
Byrd Baylor	David Macaulay
Jan Brett	Bill Martin Jr.
Eve Bunting	Robert Munsch
Eric Carle	Laura Numeroff
Lynn Cherry	Patricia Polacco
Alexandra Day	Jon Sczieska/Lane Smith
Tomie de Paola	Maurice Sendak
Lois Ehlert	Dr. Seuss
Denise Fleming	David Shannon
Mem Fox	Janet Stevens
Gail Gibbons	Chris Van Allsburg
Ruth Heller	Don and Audrey Woods
Pat Hutchins	Jane Yolen
Steven Kellogg	Ed Young

Favorite Picture Books by Content Area

Poetry
Favorite Authors: Jeff Moss, Jack Prelutsky, Shel Silverstein, Lee Bennett Hopkins, Myra Cohn Livingston, Langston Hughes

Language Arts
Agee, John
Go Hang A Salami! I'm a Lasagna Hog
Palindromes

Ahlberg, Janet and Allen
The Jolly Postman books
Writing letters, fairy tales

Bunting, Eve
The Wednesday Surprise
Literacy

Day, Alexandra
Frank and Ernest books
Using and creating career jargon

Day, Alexandra
Good Dog Carl books
Writing text to wordless picture books

Fox, Mem
Wilfred Gordon McDonald Partridge
Memoirs, family stories

Gwynne, Fred
The King Who Rained, A Chocolate Moose for Dinner, The Sixteen Hand Horse, A Little Pigeon Toad
Homonyms

Heide, Florence
The Day of Ahmed's Secret
Writing your name

Heller, Ruth
Kites Sail High, A Cache of Jewels, Many Luscious Lollipops, Merry-Go-Round, Mine, All Mine
Parts of speech

Martin Jr., Bill
Chicka, Chicka, Boom, Boom
Alphabet

Nixon, Joan Lowery
If You Were a Writer
Suggestions for writing creative material

Scieszka, Jon
The True Story of the Three Little Pigs, The Stinky Cheeseman and Other Fairly Stupid Tales
Fractured fairy tales

Steig, William
CDB
Phonetic spellings to decode pictures (higher-level problem solving)

Van Allsburg, Chris
The Mysteries of Harris Burdick
Writing stories for captions of pictures

Yolen, Jane
Owl Moon
Descriptive language: setting

Math Books
Axelrod, Amy
Pigs Will Be Pigs, Pigs on a Blanket
Money, time, odds of winning

Carle, Eric
Roosters Off to See the World, The Grouchy Ladybug, The Very Hungry Caterpillar
Numbers and sets, time, days of the week, counting

Crews, Donald
Ten Black Dots
Counting

Freyman, Saxton
One Lonely Seahorse
Counting

Greehan, Wayne
Sir Cumference and the Dragon: Pi
Circumference, radius, pi

Grossman, Bill
My Little Sister Ate One Hare
Counting

Martin Jr., Bill
Bear, Brown Bear, What Do You See? Polar Bear, Polar Bear, What Do You Hear?
Colors, sounds, animals

McGinley-Nally, Sharon
Pigs in the Pantry, Pigs Go to Market
Measurement, money

Princzes, Elinor
One Hundred Hungry Ants, A Remainder of One
Counting to one hundred, subtraction

Schwartz, David
How Much Is a Million?
Numerals, counting

Sczieska, Jon
Math Curse
Problem solving

Slate, Joseph
Miss Bindergarten Celebrates the 100th Day of Kindergarten
one hundred days of school

Wells, Rosemary
Bunny Money
Counting money

Science
Any: Jim Arnosky, Eric Carle, Gail Gibbons, Lynn Cherry, Lois Ehlert, Magic School Bus Series

Ruth Heller
Colors, Animals Born Alive and Well, Chickens Aren't the Only Ones

Loreen Leedy
Postcards from Pluto

Social Studies
Any Eve Bunting
Subjects: homeless, migrant workers, immigration, Vietnam wall, LA riots, nursing homes

APPALACHIAN REGION
Houston, Gloria
The Year of the Perfect Christmas Tree

Mills, Lauren
The Rag Coat

Rylant, Cynthia
Appalachia

EXPLORATION, EARLY AMERICA
Lyon, George Ella
Dream Place (Anasazi), *Who Came Down That Road*

Yolen, Jane
Encounter (Columbus)

Johnson, Tony
The Quilt Story

COLONIES, PILGRIMS, PRE-REVOLUTIONARY WAR
Christiansen, Candace
Calico and Tin Horns

Harness, Cheryl
Three Young Pilgrims

San Souci, Robert
N.C. Wyeth's Pilgrim

Waters, Kate
Sarah Morton's Day

CIVIL WAR, SLAVERY, BLACK HISTORY
Coles, Robert
Ruby Bridges

Golenbock, Peter
Teammates

Hopkinson, Deborah
Sweet Clara and the Freedom Quilt

Lyon, George Ella
Cecil's Story

Ringold, Faith
Aunt Harriet's Underground Railroad in the Sky

Turner, Ann
Nettie's Trip South

Winter, Jeanette
Follow the Drinking Gourd

WORLD WAR II
Coerr, Elenor
Sadako

Houston, Gloria
But No Candy

Innocenti, Robert
Blanche Rose

Mochizuki, Ken
Baseball Saved Us

Tsuchiya, Yukio
Faithful Elephants

Ziefert, Harriet
A New Coat for Anna

Novels and Class Literature Sets by Genre

Fantasy
Avi
The Poppy series: *Ragweed, Poppy, Poppy and Rye, Ereth's Birthday*

Banks, Lynn Reid
The Indian in the Cupboard series

Dahl, Roald
The BFG, Matilda, James and the Giant Peach, Charlie and the Chocolate Factory

O'Brian, Robert
The Rats of NIMH

Norton, Mary
The Borrowers

White, E.B.
Charlotte's Web,

Realistic Fiction
Bauer, Marion Dane
On My Honor

Cleary, Beverly
Dear Mr. Henshaw

DiCamillo, Kate
Because of Winn Dixie

Gardner, John Reynolds
Stone Fox

Naylor, Phyllis Reynolds
Shiloh

Paterson, Katherine
Bridge to Terabithia

Paterson, Katherine
The Great Gilly Hopkins

Paulsen, Gary
Hatchet

Rawls, Wilson
Where the Red Fern Grows

Rylant, Cynthia
Missing May

Speare, Elizabeth George
My Side of the Mountain series: *My Side of the Mountain, Far Side of the Mountain, Frightful's Mountain*

Spinelli, Jerry
Maniac Magee

Multicultural
Armstrong, William H.
Sounder

Denenberg, Barry
Stealing Home Jackie Robinson

Lord, Bette Bao
The Year of the Boar and Jackie Robinson

Slote, Alfred
Finding Buck McHenry

Taylor, Mildred D.
Roll of Thunder, Hear My Cry, Mississippi Bridge, The Well, The Friendship, The Gold Cadillac, Let the Circle Be Unbroken

Walter, Mildred Pitts
Justin and the Best Biscuits in the World

Historical Fiction
COLONIAL PERIOD
Hall, Elvajean
Margaret Pumphrey's Pilgrim Stories

Lawson, Robert
Ben and Me

Speare, Elizabeth George
The Sign of the Beaver

Speare, Elizabeth George
The Witch of Blackbird Pond

REVOLUTIONARY WAR
Archer, Jules
They Made a Revolution

Avi
The Fighting Ground

Collier, James Lincoln and Christopher
War Comes to Willy Freedom

Forbes, Esther
Johnny Tremain

Fritz, Jean
Traitor: Case of Benedict Arnold

McGovern, Ann
The Secret Soldier

BIRTH OF AMERICA
Avi
The True Confessions of Charlotte Doyle

Blos, Joan W.
A Gathering of Days

Latham, Jean Lee
Carry On, Mr. Bowditch

MacLachlan, Patricia
Sarah, Plain and Tall

Wilder, Laura Ingalls
Little House series

Civil War
Beatty, Patricia
Charley Skedaddle

Beatty, Patricia
Turn Homeward Hannah Lee, Be Ever Hopeful, Hannah Lee

Freedman, Russell
Lincoln, A Photobiography

Paulsen, Gary
Night John

Reeder, Carolyn
Shades of Gray

World War II
Frank, Anne
The Diary of Anne Frank

Fry, Varian
Assignment Rescue: The Autobiography of Varian Fry

Lowery, Lois
Number the Stars

Appendix B: Faculty and School Site Concerns Checklists

━━━━

At the same time we are setting up our classrooms, and organizing our daily accountability routines and procedures, we must also concern ourselves with becoming familiar with our new school and faculty.

Every school functions differently. Not only do we need to become aware of the federal, state, and district mandates of our school, but we also need to discover the nuances that are particular to our new school site. We need to understand the school's philosophy, procedures, and culture.

Following are detailed check lists for your use.

School Concerns

School Personnel:
- ❏ names of administrators
- ❏ names of secretaries
- ❏ secretary duties
- ❏ names of custodians
- ❏ custodian who cleans your room
- ❏ special education teachers
- ❏ guidance counselor
- ❏ Title I teachers
- ❏ ESOL teachers
- ❏ occupational therapist
- ❏ speech and hearing teachers
- ❏ gifted teachers
- ❏ school nurse

School Information:
- ❏ phone number
- ❏ address
- ❏ yearly school calendar
- ❏ map of school
- ❏ hours for students
- ❏ hours for teachers
- ❏ location of teachers lounge
- ❏ location of teachers bathroom
- ❏ school mission statement
- ❏ school pledges, songs, creeds
- ❏ fax number
- ❏ teacher phone extensions
- ❏ PTO

Union:
- ❏ school representative
- ❏ phone numbers
- ❏ benefits

Schedules:
- ❏ lunch
- ❏ lunch monitors
- ❏ labs
- ❏ planning time/special activities
- ❏ library checkout
- ❏ school events throughout year

Technology:
- ❏ copy machine procedures
- ❏ copy limits
- ❏ copy code number
- ❏ directions for using school computers
- ❏ computer passwords
- ❏ Internet and email passwords
- ❏ sending or receiving a fax
- ❏ voice mail
- ❏ homework hotline
- ❏ making long-distance phone calls
- ❏ school-used programs and templates
- ❏ scanners? printers? digital camera?

Safety Procedures:
- ❏ fire drill
- ❏ tornado/hurricane
- ❏ stranger on campus
- ❏ keeping doors locked
- ❏ keeping $ in room
- ❏ dismissal procedures
- ❏ photographing students
- ❏ visitation sign-in
- ❏ walking unescorted on campus
- ❏ emergency call button

School Concerns *(continued)*

Lab Procedures:
- ❏ limited access?
- ❏ sign-up sheet?
- ❏ person in charge of lab
- ❏ procedures for signing out materials
- ❏ what the labs contain
- ❏ aides or assistants

Charts:
- ❏ lunch seating
- ❏ assembly seating

Location of Forms:
- ❏ field trip
- ❏ attendance
- ❏ tardy slips
- ❏ discipline
- ❏ lunch count
- ❏ clinic passes
- ❏ report cards
- ❏ progress reports
- ❏ cum. folder forms
- ❏ student registration
- ❏ library book checkout permission
- ❏ ordering materials
- ❏ child study
- ❏ retained students' academic forms and assessments
- ❏ request to show a video

Other Procedures:
- ❏ cafeteria
- ❏ clinic passes
- ❏ library
- ❏ volunteering in classroom

Other Procedures cont.:
- ❏ class pets
- ❏ cooking in classroom
- ❏ recess
- ❏ candles
- ❏ dress codes
- ❏ classroom parties
- ❏ reserving school areas
- ❏ early checkout
- ❏ discipline
- ❏ parent visitation
- ❏ excused and unexcused absences

Other:

School Concerns *(continued)*

District Office:
- ❏ location and address
- ❏ phone number
- ❏ person in charge of payroll
- ❏ person in charge of recertification
- ❏ person in charge of staff development
- ❏ person in charge of insurance

Security:
- ❏ procedures for working after hours
- ❏ security code numbers
- ❏ keys to building
- ❏ keys to classroom
- ❏ name and phone number of campus security

Bookkeeping:
- ❏ name of bookkeeper
- ❏ petty cash fund for children without lunch money?
- ❏ field trip money?
- ❏ classroom miscellaneous supplies

Field Trip Procedures:
- ❏ forms
- ❏ scheduling procedures
- ❏ approval
- ❏ bus scheduler
- ❏ trip scheduler
- ❏ fingerprinting of chaperones
- ❏ students who cannot pay
- ❏ parents driving
- ❏ vehicle inspection

Field Trip Procedures cont.:
- ❏ siblings attending
- ❏ mile restrictions
- ❏ hours of school bus
- ❏ required? restricted?
- ❏ $ allotment from school or PTO
- ❏ maximum amount students can be charged per trip
- ❏ maximum number of fund-raisers allowed

Assessments:
- ❏ grading system
- ❏ benchmarks and standards
- ❏ required assessments
- ❏ location of testing materials
- ❏ location of cumulative folder
- ❏ required contents of cumulative folder
- ❏ report card and interim schedules

Lesson Plans:
- ❏ benchmarks noted?
- ❏ required format?
- ❏ nongraded?
- ❏ narrative report card?
- ❏ collected for review?

Conferences:
- ❏ required? how often?
- ❏ student-led?

Special Needs Services:
- ❏ students in class with special needs
- ❏ child study procedures
- ❏ 504 procedures

©2002 by Deborah Coughlin from *How to Plan for the School Year.* Portsmouth, NH: Heinemann.

School Concerns *(continued)*

Special Needs Services cont.:
- ❏ ESOL procedures
- ❏ Title I procedures
- ❏ gifted program
- ❏ available resources
- ❏ schedule of services
- ❏ copies of all IEPs

Classroom Materials:
- ❏ location of textbooks and consumable materials
- ❏ ordering for school year
- ❏ procedures for ordering
- ❏ yearly teacher allowance
- ❏ required textbooks
- ❏ catalogs and forms for ordering
- ❏ what materials are already ordered for this year
- ❏ using textbook $ to purchase other types of print

Morning Announcements:
- ❏ schoolwide morning announcements?
- ❏ on the TV?
- ❏ on the intercom?
- ❏ time?
- ❏ channel?
- ❏ what they contain

Location of:
- ❏ Miscellaneous
- ❏ IEPs on students
- ❏ school calendars
- ❏ school menus
- ❏ courier envelopes

Location of cont.:
- ❏ courier drop
- ❏ U.S. mail drop
- ❏ clinic
- ❏ student handbooks
- ❏ vending machines
- ❏ ice/freezer
- ❏ school master calendar
- ❏ teacher mailboxes
- ❏ smoking area
- ❏ special activities
- ❏ parent work room
- ❏ laminating room
- ❏ Ellison machine
- ❏ book binder
- ❏ textbook room
- ❏ stored furniture

Notes:

Personal Concerns

Insurance:
- [ ] health
- [ ] life
- [ ] dental
- [ ] vision
- [ ] short-term disability
- [ ] long-term disability
- [ ] sick leave bank
- [ ] personal property coverage

Certification:
- [ ] requirements
- [ ] renewal requirements
- [ ] beginning teacher requirements
- [ ] teacher evaluations

Professional Growth:
- [ ] monies available for conferences
- [ ] professional time off for conferences
- [ ] monies available for graduate school
- [ ] district staff development opportunities

Always Know the Location of:
- [ ] your certificate
- [ ] faculty handbook
- [ ] district handbook
- [ ] yearly contract
- [ ] grade-level benchmarks and standards
- [ ] required assessment scores
- [ ] completed required paperwork
- [ ] your keys

Payroll:
- [ ] salary
- [ ] schedule of pay periods
- [ ] paid over summer?
- [ ] retirement plan?
- [ ] IRAs?
- [ ] automatic deductions
- [ ] automatic deposits

Time Off:
- [ ] number of sick days
- [ ] number of personal days
- [ ] procedures for calling in sick
- [ ] procedures for taking personal days
- [ ] accruing comp time
- [ ] policy on days off directly before or after a holiday break
- [ ] location of required forms

Other:

Appendix C: Chapter Forms

Class Attendance Form															
Week	Week _____					Week _____					Week _____				
Day	M	T	W	T	F	M	T	W	T	F	M	T	W	T	F
Date															
Assignment *or* Attendance															
Name															

Sample Weekly Lesson Plan

Month:	Monday	Tuesday	Wednesday
8:15–8:30	Morning procedures		
8:30–8:50	Journals, announcements, attendance, lunch count, read or write when done		
8:50–9:15	Calendar, Mr. Bear, Helper Share Time		
9:15–10:40 Language Arts		10:10 - Library: Checkout Only	
10:40–10:55	Clean up supplies and room, get materials needed for lunch, take lunch boxes to specials		
10:55–11:35 Specials	Music P.2	PE on blacktop	Art
11:41–12:06	LUNCH		
12:06–12:45	Recess	Recess	Recess
12:45–1:15	Bathrooms, water, read-aloud, snack	Bathrooms, water, read-aloud, snack	Bathrooms, water, read-aloud, snack
1:15–1:45		Keyboards	
1:45–2:15			
2:15–2:30	Put away all materials in cubbies, ready for home, do classroom jobs		
2:30–2:50	Read on carpet until dismissal		
2:50–3:00	Dismissal		
3:00–3:15	Outside duty: West Circle, North End		
3:15–4:00			Faculty

Sample Weekly Lesson Plan *(continued)*

Month:	Thursday	Friday	Notes:
8:15–8:30	Morning procedures		
8:30–8:50	Journals, announcements, attendance, lunch count, read or write when done		
8:50–9:15	Calendar, Mr. Bear, Helper Share Time		
9:15–10:40 Language Arts			
10:40–10:55	Clean up supplies and room, get materials needed for lunch, take lunch boxes to specials		
10:55–11:35	Guidance	PE	
11:41–12:06	LUNCH		
12:06–12:45	Recess	Recess	
12:45–1:15	Bathrooms, water, read-aloud, snack	Bathrooms, water, read-aloud, snack	
1:15–1:45	Black box (1:20–2:00)		
1:45–2:15			
2:15–2:30	Put away all materials in cubbies, ready for home, do classroom jobs		
2:30–2:50	Read on carpet until dismissal		
2:50–3:00	Dismissal		
3:00–3:15	Outside duty: West Circle, North End		
3:15–4:00			

CLASS JOBS	NAME
Put away lunch magnets	
Return library books	
Date sign-in sheet	
Ready calendar for tomorrow	
Feed Rose	
Water plants	
Put away chairs	
End of line	
Escort	
Door Holder	
Pass out papers	
Pick up the carpet area	
Clean up the wet area	
Organize envelope books	
Table checker	
Cubbie checker	
Organize science center	
Trash can monitor	
Puppets	
Language arts area	
Felt story area	
Class library	
White board	
Pick up the floor	

Reading Objectives and Goals

The student:

- ❏ reads for a variety of purposes—enjoyment, socialization/inclusion, to locate and retrieve information, to learn, to share and discuss, to gather ideas for writing, to provide structures for writing
- ❏ constructs meaning
- ❏ turns to text to verify, clarify, confirm, and explore
- ❏ connects story to personal experience
- ❏ connects story to other stories
- ❏ uses prior knowledge and experiences when reading
- ❏ makes predictions about text
- ❏ knows how to hold, open, and read a book from left to right
- ❏ reads phonetically
- ❏ uses context for unfamiliar words
- ❏ sees relationships between characters
- ❏ identifies characters, setting, and plot or main idea
- ❏ identifies tone or mood of the story
- ❏ discusses beyond a literal level
- ❏ summarizes
- ❏ retells
- ❏ sequences
- ❏ recognizes words we read daily
- ❏ asks for clarification
- ❏ self-corrects
- ❏ understands cause and effect
- ❏ understands fact/fiction
- ❏ understands fact/opinion
- ❏ understands fantasy/reality
- ❏ uses picture clues
- ❏ highlights difficult or new words
- ❏ makes notes, drawings, or diagrams
- ❏ critiques various texts
- ❏ identifies the work of several authors and/or illustrators
- ❏ selects books independently
- ❏ recalls what is read
- ❏ initiates a book discussion
- ❏ considers differences of opinion
- ❏ identifies and participates in repeated text
- ❏ identifies rhyme
- ❏ shares thinking with others
- ❏ searches for patterns in reading and language
- ❏ rereads for meaning
- ❏ skims
- ❏ reads silently
- ❏ shows pleasure from reading
- ❏ reads a variety of genres
- ❏ reads orally with fluency
- ❏ reads orally with expression
- ❏ chooses to read
- ❏ locates and extracts details and words from text
- ❏ reads what is considered grade-level material

Intermediate Literature Group Contract

Literature discussion groups meet on Mondays, Wednesdays, and Fridays. This contract reflects the pages to be read for each day's discussion. After reading, you are also responsible for responding to the book in writing and sharing this response with your literature group.

Between the dates of _____ and _____,

I agree to read the book titled: _____

_____.

I will pace myself according to this contract.

Monday	Wednesday	Friday

Student's signature: _____

Teacher's signature: _____

Parent's signature: _____

Intermediate Reading Journal Assignment

Your reading journal assignment for each day is "free discussion." Listed below are discussion topics. You may choose among these topics or create your own. Do not repeat topic assignments within the same book. Date each entry and write the number of the topic you are responding to.
EXAMPLE: March 1st–Day 1

TOPIC CHOICES:

1. Talk about characters and their qualities.

2. Compare characters within the story.

3. Compare a character in one book with a character in another book.

4. Explain why a character or the story is meaningful to you.

5. Discuss a quote from the book that is meaningful to you.

6. Talk about why you think the author wrote this book.

7. Describe the problem your main character faces and predict how he or she will solve it.

8. Talk about what you think will happen next.

9. Discuss your impressions of the book.

10. Pick out phrases that demonstrate the author's use of colorful language.

11. Find five sentences that tell about the setting. Choose one of these sentences and draw a picture based upon the author's description.

12. Find sentences from the book that describe what the characters look like.

13. Do you agree with what the character is doing? Would you behave the same or differently? Why?

14. Which character is most like you? Why?

15. It is your job to prepare a keepsake box for one of the main characters. Choose a character. Pick five items you would place in the box. Talk about why you chose these items.

16. Create a story map. Include characters, setting, conflict, and solution.

17. If you were the author, what would you change?

Reading Journal Assignment *(continued)*

18. What is the mood of this book? How does the author help create this mood? (Look at use of language, plot, and setting.)

19. Is this book fiction or nonfiction? How do you know? Give examples.

20. Is this book similar to other books your author has written? Does your author use similar elements in his or her stories? Can you determine the author's writing style?

21. Record new vocabulary. Discuss how you determined the word's meaning.

22. Summarize the reading section.

23. Which character would you most want for a friend? Why?

24. Discuss an example of where the author is "showing" not "telling."

25. Would you want to be the main character? Why?

26. Could this story take place in another time or place? Why?

27. Ask the author a question that you answer yourself.

28. How has this book helped you learn more about this time period? What was new or interesting to you?

29. List, in order, the main events of the story.

30. You are one of the main characters. Record this reading selection as an entry in your diary.

31. Who is telling this story? How would this story be different if told from another character's point of view?

32. If you could change one thing in the book, what would it be? Why?

33. If one of the characters were an animal, what would she or he be? Why?

34.

35.

Intermediate Literature Group Checklist

Week of:

NAME	Read	Journaled	Shared	Listened	Notes

Reading Group Self-Evaluation

	Strengths	Weaknesses
Reading		
Listening		
Responding		
Sharing		

Primary Reading Contract

Name: _____

Date: _____

Homework for each day below is to read your reading book and complete one of the chosen reading assignments below. We will meet in reading groups on Monday, Wednesday, and Friday to discuss the book and share our projects.

Mon. I have read the book _____

I have completed an assignment _____

Parent signature _____

Wed. I have read the book _____

I have completed an assignment _____

Parent signature _____

Fri. I have read the book _____

I have completed an assignment _____

Parent signature _____

ASSIGNMENT CHOICES

1. Draw a picture about the story.
2. Write about the story.
3. Create an art project about the story.
4. Write a poem about the story.
5. Create a dictionary of new words found in the story.
6. Pick out your favorite page to read.
7. Write a song about the story.
8. Dress like one of the characters.

continued on next page

Primary Reading Contract *(continued)*

ASSIGNMENT CHOICES *(CONTINUED)*

9. Draw, write, and/or create something about the characters or setting.
10. Discuss the order of the story. What happened first, second, third?
11. Make up your own story based on this one.
12. Make up your own story by changing the ending, characters, or setting.
13. Put characters from another story into this story. What would this new story be like?
14. What do you notice in the book?
15. How would this story be different if an event in the story changed?
16. Create something that this story makes you think of, wonder, or imagine.
17. Talk about another story this book reminds you of.
18. Create a new story using the same characters.
19. Create a new chapter for the book.
20. Act out the story.
21. Create puppets for the story.
22. Summarize or retell the story.
23. Make a mobile about the story.
24. Make a picture time line of the story.
25. Create a map of the setting.
26. Research any of the characters or places in the story.
27. Make a diorama.
28. Use magazines and make a collage or picture of the story.
29. Make a list of rhyming words based on a couple of words from the story.
30. Look for your spelling words in the book.
31. Pick out compound words from the story.
32. Pick out contractions from the story.
33. Talk about your favorite part of the story.
34. Bake something to do with the story.

Think of your own suggestions:

35.

36.

37.

Literature Sets Ballot

Write your first, second, and third book choice very clearly. Do not forget to sign your name.

First Choice _____

Second Choice _____

Third Choice _____

_____
Name

Envelope Book Parent Letter

Dear Parents,

   Throughout the year your child will be bringing home an envelope containing one or more books (an envelope book) with which to practice reading at home. Although I have selected the level of difficulty for instructional purposes, it takes a while to reach an optimal level for each child. Initially, the books your child brings home may be too easy or too hard.

   Please help your child read the books. On the envelope form write the title and date. After reading the book, fill in the column indicating practice level. Also, your written comments from time to time will help us communicate throughout the year.

   When the envelope is brought back to school, I will listen to your child read the story. I will assist in developing appropriate reading strategies and help in selecting new books to bring home. I don't expect the envelope books to be returned each day, but try to have them back at least once a week.

   Please keep in mind that reading is a strategic process. Predicting, making mistakes, self-correcting, and confirming are part of the process. Familiarity, repetition, and rhyme help children become successful readers. Here are a few ideas to help you support your child's reading:

- Read the book to your child first or read along with her or him.
- Encourage your child to point to the words.
- Encourage your child to use the pictures and beginning letter when reading.
- Talk about the story. Ask your child to predict what the story might be about and what might happen next. When your child comes to a word he or she doesn't know, suggest reading to the end of the sentence . . . [second page not available]

Envelope Book Cover Sheet

This Envelope Book Belongs To

_____

In Dr. Coughlin's First Grade Class
Unit G
Hans Christian Andersen Elementary

Please practice reading this book every night. Return it to school every day in this envelope. When ready, read your book to your teacher, class, reading buddy, or parent helper.
Write the title of the book on your
<u>Books I Have Read Sheet.</u>
Choose another book to practice.

Envelope Book: Books I Have Read Sheet	
Date:	
Name:	
BOOKS I HAVE READ	**Book Number**

Envelope Book Weekly Checklist

Envelope Books

Name: **Week of:**

Monday	Level #	Parent Signature:	Title:
Tuesday	Level #	Parent Signature:	Title:
Wednesday	Level #	Parent Signature:	Title:
Thursday	Level #	Parent Signature:	Title:
Friday	Level #	Parent Signature:	Title:

Comments:

Writing Workshop Objectives and Goals

The student:
- ❏ chooses and develops a topic
- ❏ has a sense of audience
- ❏ uses text cues: charts, graphs, maps
- ❏ shares writing
- ❏ shows growth in story length and development
- ❏ revises
- ❏ edits
- ❏ rewrites
- ❏ publishes
- ❏ creates stories with a beginning, middle, and end
- ❏ uses other printed materials for writing ideas
- ❏ uses other printed materials to locate conventional spelling
- ❏ uses correct spacing (between letters, between words)
- ❏ writes legibly
- ❏ forms letters correctly
- ❏ writes phonetically
- ❏ utilizes conventions _____% of the time in writing

- ❏ uses descriptive language
- ❏ uses reference sources
- ❏ uses prewriting strategies of webbing, outlining, brainstorming
- ❏ is moving from invented spellings to conventional spellings
- ❏ chooses to write
- ❏ indents paragraphs
- ❏ utilizes consistent use of tense
- ❏ writes cohesive pieces
- ❏ can read her or his own stories
- ❏ writes in a variety of genres
- ❏ uses age-appropriate vocabulary
- ❏ uses age-appropriate sentence structure
- ❏ demonstrates a sense of voice
- ❏ takes risks
- ❏ draws more than writes
- ❏ utilizes print for a variety of reasons
- ❏ writes on the correct side of the paper
- ❏ utilizes characters, settings, and plot

Writing Workshop Procedures (Primary)

Author and Illustrator: _____

Writing Workshop Procedures

1. Date your paper.

2. Write something every day. Use your ear spelling and try your personal best. Don't worry. We will edit your story for spelling later.

3. Draw and color a picture for your story.

4. Be ready to share your writing during Author's Circle.

Writing Workshop Procedures (Intermediate)

Writing Workshop

1. Mark only one line through changes.

2. Don't erase.

3. Write the date on every piece.

4. Write your name on every piece.

5. Write daily.

6. Save everything.

7. Do your personal best.

Writing Workshop Status Checklist

Status Check

Name	Monday	Tuesday	Wednesday	Thursday	Friday

Science Observation Procedures

Scientist: _____

1. Date your paper.

2. Look at the object we are observing.

3. Complete your Science Observation form.

4. Draw and color the object observed so that it looks exactly like it is now.

5. Fasten your completed observation form to the back of your observation log.

6. Take your time and do your personal best. Write neatly and slowly.

Science Observation Form

SCIENTIST:

PROPERTIES:

ITEM:

Color

DATE:

Size

❑ Living and Alive
❑ Living but Dead
❑ Non Living

Shape

Weight

PICTURE:

Texture

Mr. Bear Letter

Dear Boys and Girls,   August

I am so glad that school has started because Mrs. Coughlin has suggested that I take turns spending the night with you. I've been living at her house since she bought me this summer.

I like living at the Coughlins' house, but there isn't a lot of action. Mrs. Coughlin's husband, Dan, and his classroom cockatoo named Fermie live there. But her daughter, Kelly, only comes home to visit once in a while. Kelly goes to college in Florida, where Mr. and Mrs. Coughlin once lived. Mrs. Coughlin goes to college also. She is finishing her doctorate and therefore does not spend very much time playing with me. It can get very lonely.

I will take turns visiting you, so be sure to bring me back to school each day. The first time you take me home, please help me tell about your family. Also, I love bedtime stories. I hope you will read me one.

Your Pal,
Mr. Bear

Mr. Bear Form

Name: _____

Date: _____

The story I read to Mr. Bear was

_____

It had _____ pages.

I read to him in _____.

He (liked) (didn't like) the story.

This is a picture of our favorite part:

Language Arts and Reading Area Supplies

Magnetic letters
Cookie cutter letters
Play dough
Alphabet stamps
Cookie sheets
Dry-erase markers
Magnetic white boards
Chalkboards
White boards
Leveled books
Library books
Theme books
Handmade paper books
Blank audiotapes
Stories on tape
Cassette player
Listening center
Magazines
Newspapers
Scrabble
Letter tiles
Word walls
Felt boards
Felt story manipulatives
Puppets
Storybook characters
Storybook character/book
Backpacks

Mr. Bear folder
Mr. Bear forms
Envelope book forms
Magnetic words
Magnetic onsets
Magnetic rhymes
Sight word cards
Big books
Picture books
Poetry books
Rocking chair
Pillows
Couch
Carpets
Author's chair
Nonfiction books
Phonemic awareness and
    sight word games
I Spy and *Hidden Picture*
    books (builds sight words in
    isolation)
Sentence strips
Calendar
Mailbox
Classroom charts, poems,
    posters

Science Area Supplies

Color Paddles
Bird nests
Bones/animal skulls
Magnifying glasses
Microscopes
Shells
Seeds
Plants
Ant farm
Fish
Snake skin
Rocks
Petrified wood
Cotton plant
Balancing scales
Magnets
Planet space ball
Marble/chute games
Teeth
Science books

Animal puppets
Pinecones
Corn stalk
Handheld microscopes
Nature journals
Globe
Roots
Leaves
Bug box
Butterfly net
Measuring tapes
Bathroom scale
Clipboards
Science Observation forms
Bird feathers
Gyroscope
Preserved brain, preserved
  snakes, etc.
X-rays

Art and Writing Workshop Area Supplies

Assorted construction paper
Wallpaper
Magazines
Address books (sports teams, musicians, TV stars, businesses, politicians, etc.)
ZIP code books
Assorted tissue paper
Empty boxes, containers, lids for recycled art sculptures
Clay
Play dough
Watercolors
Dry-erase markers
Colored chalk
Stencils
White boards
Chalkboards
Markers
Alphabet markers
Stamp design markers
Crayons
Colored pencils
Scissors
Tape
Glue
Glue stick
Permanent markers
Fabric
Miscellaneous craft materials: beads, sequins, google eyes
Craft sticks
How to Draw Books
Lace
Brown paper lunch bags
White paper lunch bags
Wax paper
Paper plates
Paper cups (for painting)
Scrap materials box
Brads (paper fasteners)

Used file folders
Staplers
Tape
Paper clips
Date stamp
Ink pad
Newsprint paper
White copy paper
Lined newsprint paper
Notebook paper
Envelopes
Stationery
Used greeting cards
Felt
Cardboard
Roll of white paper
Paint shirts
Pipe cleaners
Class mailing stamps
Postcards
Pencils
Erasers
Dictionaries
Writing prompts/ideas
Story starters
Thesaurus
Word banks (color words, number words, family words, theme words, etc.)
ABC handwriting tape or models
Writing workshop notebooks
Writing workshop portfolios (for big works in progress)
Writing workshop procedures
Pencil sharpeners
Stickie notes
Feathers
Highlighters
Handheld spell checker
Library of student writings

Math Area Supplies

Geoboards
Rubber bands
Math calendar
Paper money and coins
Snap™ Cubes
Snap™ Rods
Cash register
Calculators
Rulers
Counters
Sorting materials
Pattern blocks
Mirrors (symmetry)
Building materials
Base ten blocks
Pattern strips
Puzzles
Measuring tape
Measuring cups
Measuring spoons

Various size containers (volume)
Bathroom scale
Kitchen scale
Outside thermometer
Inside thermometer
Plastic or cardboard clocks
Weaving materials
Graphing chart
Games:
  Yahtzee™
  Memory games
  Candyland™
  Chutes and Ladders™
  Dice
  Battleship™
  Chess
  Checkers
  3D geometric shapes
  Maps
  Card games

Student-Led Conference Family Night:
Letter to Parents

Date _____

Dear _____,

    Please come to my student-led conference family night!

    It is on _____

between _____ o'clock and _____ o'clock.

    We can attend at any time that is convenient. I will show you around the classroom and show you what I am learning at school.

    My teacher, _____,
is looking forward to seeing you, too.

Love,

_____

Student-Led Conference Sample Agenda 1

Student:

Parent(s):

CENTERS:

Reading	Journal
Words	Math
Science	Talk with Dr. Coughlin

Refreshments

Activity Center	Comments
READING: Read the book you have been practicing for your family What is the title? What is the level? Share other books that you have read.	Student:
QUESTION AND SUGGESTIONS FOR PARENTS: How are you doing with your reading? How did you know that word was _____? Can you find the word _____ in the story? What is your favorite part? Why? What do you plan on reading next?	Parent:

Student-Led Conference Sample Agenda 1 *(continued)*

Activity Center	Comments
JOURNAL: Share your journal with your family. Write a new entry with them tonight. Tonight, write and draw about your favorite part of *Charlotte's Web.*	Student:
QUESTION AND SUGGESTIONS FOR PARENTS: Does your child write daily? Is each paper dated? Contain a drawing? Contain writing? Ask him or her to try his or her ear spelling when he or she spells. Does your child know his or her sounds? Does your child use capitalization or punctuation? Does your child write letters, sounds, words, or sentences? Can he or she talk about the story *Charlotte's Web*?	Parent:
WORDS: Create the alphabet using magnetic letters. Find the O and W. Make as many OW words as you can. If time allows, create your name, write words you know, and make new words from words you know.	Student:
QUESTION AND SUGGESTIONS FOR PARENTS: How comfortable is your child with letter recognition and sounds? Can he or she create words from known words? Help him or her by switching letters around and creating new words.	Parent:

Student-Led Conference Sample Agenda 1 *(continued)*

Activity Center	Comments
MATH: Write your numbers as far as you can go. (Stop at 100!) Next, count the straws on the table. How many tens? _____ How many ones?_____ How many straws are on the table? _____	Student:
QUESTIONS AND SUGGESTIONS FOR PARENTS: Olders should be able to write at least up to 20. Youngers should be able to write to 10. Watch for reversals. This is common. To help your child with the straws, ask "how many bundles of ten" there are. Start with the tens and count up with the ones.	Parent:
SCIENCE: Share your cow book and drafts with your family. Next, share the book *The Milk Makers* and discuss what you have learned about cows and the dairy.	Student:
QUESTIONS AND SUGGESTIONS FOR PARENTS: After reading *The Milk Makers* we wrote facts that we learned. Each child picked three facts and copied them onto cards. Each fact card was then put on each page of the child's book. Our list of class facts is hanging on the easel. Ask your child to share these with you. Ask your child about CUD!	Parent:
Visit with Dr. Coughlin	
Refreshments	

Student-Led Conference Sample Agenda 2

February 22nd and February 24th

Child's Name _____

Date _____

Procedure: Travel and move to any empty table you desire. You may do as many stations as you want, but be sure one of your stops is Dr. Coughlin. Fill out your conference form at each station.

1. Make an animal track out of clay. What track did you make?

2. How many ways can you make a quarter? List them. (P=Penny, N=Nickel, D=Dime, Q=Quarter)

3. Share what you know about owls. What are some facts that you talked about?

4. Share the owl pellet with your family. Include your Science Observation. What are owl pellets? What did you find inside? Use the back as needed.

5. Share your favorite owl book and/or poem.

6. Visit with Dr. Coughlin about your Young Author story.

Sample Newsletter

Coughlin Class Newsletter and Update
Dr. Coughlin - First Grade - Unit 6
Hans Christian Andersen Elementary School

Interim Reports   First Quarter   September 14, 2001

Dear Families,

Welcome to the middle of our first school quarter. In the past four weeks we have spent a great deal of time reviewing basic skills from kindergarten, establishing procedures and expectations, modeling and practicing regular curricular routines, establishing and learning first grade behaviors and responsibilities, and working towards the creation of a caring, respectful, safe, risk-free, nurturing learning environment.

In the meantime, I have been getting to know and learn the children so that I can better meet their academic, personal, and social needs. We have also completed all of the district's first grade baseline testing requirements in the language arts and mathematics. These assessments were used in combination with classroom work samples, behaviors, and observations to achieve this quarter's interim report.

Interim Reports: Adequate Progress vs. Not Adequate Progress

The district's baseline testing is very specific as to what scores constitute *on grade level, below grade level,* and *substantially deficient* work. Children who score below grade level, or substantially deficient on any of the baseline measures are not considered to be making adequate progress at this time.

Additionally, I am also watchful, concerned, and interested in the progress and work samples of the children who scored within one or two points of the *grade level* cut-off. Usually a child's work samples and classroom observations will help confirm or contrast the tested scores. However, because this is review work, and until I know the children better, I am marking any child who scored below the cut-off, or within one or two points of the cut-off as *Not Adequate Progress.*

What Does It Mean?

Interim reports are not necessarily a reflection of your child's future career or performance in first grade. Remember: Your child is learning. Everything we do is new and/or practice.

First grade is different than kindergarten in that the children must now conform to more stringent classroom behaviors, responsibilities, independence, and academic rigor. Listening, and establishing sound learning behaviors are vital to your child's success in school. This is not easy for young children. After all, they *are* children. They should want to play and visit—and they have not had much experience in their educational careers to truly understand their job of school. The first interim report is a way of concretely establishing first grade academic and behavioral expectations. We can build on the positive while working on areas that are self-defeating before they become embedded as bad habits.

Sample Newsletter *(continued)*

Conferences:

Please use your parent journals to contact me regarding a conference. I would like to meet with as many families as possible. I would also like your child to join our conference so we can all maintain input, understanding, ownership, and responsibility.

If there is an issue that is inappropriate or uncomfortable to discuss in front of your child, then we certainly need to meet in private. Just let me know.

Domino's Pizza Fund-Raiser:

Pizza cards and the money collected was due on Friday, September 14th. If you have not done so, please return your fund-raiser card and money ASAP. We need to order the cards for distribution. Remember: the money will be used for first grade field trips.

Class Update:

Over the weekend I will create a parent letter that will go home on Monday.

The letter will identify class procedures (which have changed and/or been modified frequently as needed) and a rough outline of our yearly curriculum and studies.

Attached to the letter will be a list of skills and content that can be practiced at home, as well as a list of the 300 most commonly used words in children's writing and vocabulary. These words should become sight words (readily identified) by your child throughout the year.

"The child is not GOING to be someone. . . . The child already IS someone."
Emsy Dunn

Thank you for your continued support.

Please let me know if there is anything that I can do. I look forward to meeting with you shortly.

Sincerely,
Dr. Coughlin

P.S. I would like to have an *Open House Family Night* for the purposes of modeling ways to help your child at home in the area of the language arts. If you would be interested in attending such an evening, please let me know.

Also, a reminder—please send in a baby picture for a class project next week. It will be returned unharmed.

Form 3a Classroom Map

Sketch doors, windows, shelves, bulletin boards, white boards, chalkboards, and outlets

Form 3b Notes and Brainstorms

Wall Space

Colors

Arrangement Ideas

Form 3c Classroom Needs List

Extension cords, wall mountings, plants, outlet adapters, rugs, furniture, storage tubs, wall hooks, etc.

Wish List:

Form 3d Classroom Final Copy

Color Scheme

Main Color: Wall Colors: Fabric Colors:

Secondary Colors: Carpet Colors: Color of Chairs:

Window Measurements

1.

2.

3.

4.

Board Measurements

1.

2.

3.

4.

Curtain Measurements (Windows)

1.

2.

3.

4.

Desks or Tables?   Number of Desks   Number of Chairs

_____   _____   _____

Form 3d Classroom Final Copy *(continued)*

Curtain Measurements (Shelves)

1.

2.

3.

4.

List of Furniture I Have:

Notes:

Form 3e Classroom Shopping List

Items from a discount store:	Items from a lumber/hardware store:	Items from a grocery store:

Items from a fabric store:	Items from an educational store:	Catalogs:

Miscellaneous:

Form 3f Classroom Summary Checklist

Sketched Classroom Map:
- ❏ doors
- ❏ windows
- ❏ bulletin boards
- ❏ chalkboards
- ❏ white boards
- ❏ shelving
- ❏ outlets & cords
- ❏ Checked for convenience
- ❏ Checked for safety factors
- ❏ Planned wall space
- ❏ Measured boards
- ❏ Measured windows
- ❏ Measured curtains
- ❏ Counted chairs
- ❏ Counted tables
- ❏ Took furniture inventory

- ❏ Chose colors
- ❏ Set up centers and areas
- ❏ Made shelf and bookcase curtains
- ❏ Created shopping list
- ❏ Created needs/wish list
- ❏ Cleaned the room
- ❏ Moved large furniture into classroom
- ❏ Arranged the room
- ❏ Moved in remaining furniture
- ❏ Organized files
- ❏ Organized books
- ❏ Completed setting up classroom
- ❏ Added finishing touches
- ❏ Added labels

Notes:

Form 4a First Day of School
Child Information Form

Child's Name: _____

Parent's Name: _____

Where can you be reached today? _____

Phone Numbers:

Home: _____ Work: _____

Beeper: _____ Cell: _____

Emergency: _____

How is your child getting home today?

Bus number _____ I am picking up at door _____ Car rider _____

I am picking up at _____ Sibling picking up at door _____ Walker _____

Daycare van _____ After care at school _____

What is child doing for lunch today? _____

Brought lunch from home _____ Needs to buy milk _____

Getting lunch at school with account number _____

Buying lunch at school with cash _____

Where is your child's lunch money? _____

Does your child have medicine in the clinic? _____

Instructions: _____

_____

What else do I need to know today? _____

_____

_____

_____

Form 4b Parent Information Form

Please print. Thank you.

Child's name: _____

Parent's name: _____

Child's age and birth date: _____

Child's nickname: _____

Child's home address: _____

Child's mailing address: _____

Home phone:_____ Work phone:_____

Cell phone:_____ Beeper: _____

Email address: _____

Emergency contact and phone number: _____

Medications, allergies, special needs? _____

_____

_____

What goals do you have for your child this school year?_____

_____

_____

_____

In which ways would you like to volunteer and/or assist the classroom? Working in the school setting? Working on projects at home? Is there anything you would especially like to assist with or present?_____

_____

_____

On the back: Please share with me any other information that you feel I should know about your child.

Form 4c Child/Parent Information Summary Checklist

❑ First Day of School Child Information Form
❑ Parent Information Form
❑ Parent Letter
❑ Class Recording Sheet
❑ Student Information Sheet
❑ Class Supply List

Beginning of the Year Forms are Copied
  ❑ Literature Contracts
  ❑ Writing Workshop Status Checklist
  ❑ Science Observation Forms
  ❑ Mr. Bear Form
  ❑ Weekly Job Chart
  ❑ Weekly Behavior Chart
  ❑ Other:
  ❑ Other:
  ❑ Other:
❑ Made Lunch Number Clothespins
❑ Made Voting for Lunch Headings for Cookies Sheet

Made Journals
  ❑ Math
  ❑ Morning
  ❑ Science
  ❑ Other:
  ❑ Other:
  ❑ Other:
❑ Made Weekly Folders
❑ Laminated Folders
❑ Made Helper Calendar
❑ Created Weekly Job Chart
❑ Created Student Record Folders
❑ Created Student Working Portfolios
❑ Created Record-Keeping Notebook
❑ Created Assessment Notebook
❑ Created Writing Workshop Portfolios
❑ Gathered Miscellaneous Assessments
❑ Arranged Student Seating
❑ Made Nametags
❑ Made Hall Passes
❑ Created Class Procedures
❑ Stocked Classroom

Notes:

Form 4d Classroom Shopping List

❏ spring clothespins
❏ business card magnets
❏ blank business cards
❏ cookie sheets
❏ manilla file folders
❏ metal lunch box (or bucket)
❏ white copy paper
❏ tagboard
❏ heavy-duty stapler
❏ three-prong folders
❏ yearly calendar
❏ three-inch notebooks (record-keeping, assessments, plans)
❏ notebook dividers
❏ transparencies for the copier
❏ stickie notes
❏ zippered plastic bags
❏ snacks
❏ soapless hand gel
❏ dry-erase markers
❏ watercolor markers

❏ felt-tip pens
❏ black ink pens
❏ electric pencil sharpener
❏ paper cutter
❏ transparent tape
❏ masking tape
❏ rubber bands
❏ paper clips
❏ pushpins
❏ roll of magnetic tape
❏ roll of sticky Velcro
❏ three-hole punch
❏ hole punch
❏ pencils
❏ notebook paper
❏ legal pads (for notes)
❏ Band-Aids and an antibacterial cream (Keep in your desk. Paper cuts hurt and become easily infected.)

Notes:

Form 4e Student Information Form

Student Name:	Bus Num.	Lunch Num.	Student ID Num.	Phone Num.	Age & Birth date

Form 4f Blank Class Roster					
Student Name:					

Index